Jesus the Nazarene

Jesus the Nazarene

The Talmud and the Founder of Christianity

A. JORDAN

RESOURCE *Publications* · Eugene, Oregon

JESUS THE NAZARENE
The Talmud and the Founder of Christianity

Resource Publications
An Imprint of Wipf and Stock Publishers
199 W. 8th Ave., Suite 3
Eugene, OR 97401

www.wipfandstock.com

PAPERBACK ISBN: 978-1-6667-5084-3
HARDCOVER ISBN: 978-1-6667-5085-0
EBOOK ISBN: 978-1-6667-5086-7

MARCH 21, 2023 9:01 AM

Old Testament or Hebrew Bible quotations are from Tanakh: The Holy Scriptures: The New JPS Translation According to the Traditional Hebrew Text (NJPS)

New Testament quotations are from New Revised Standard Version Bible, copyright © 1989 National Council of the Churches of Christ in the United States of America. Used by permission. All rights reserved worldwide.

Talmud quotations used with permission from the Koren Talmud Bavli, the Noé Edition. Jerusalem: Koren Publishers Jerusalem, 1965, 2019.

Contents

Preface

J ESUS HAS ALWAYS FASCINATED ME; I have always wanted to know who
the real man was. I embarked on several attempts to learn about him,
both directly through the texts most associated with him, the Gospels, and
through secondary sources and historical writing on the "historical Jesus."
To find the historical man at the heart of one of the world's largest and
most influential religions seemed like a treasure hunt, with considerable
trials along the way, but with even more potential reward upon finding that
buried gold.

How to go about it? As a young man, I found a job at an independent
bookstore and took the opportunity to collect a number of books from the
Jesus Seminar, a group of scholars who wrote about the historical Jesus
and presented their findings in several books. This included scholars such
as Marcus Borg, John Dominic Crossan, and Robert Funk, among many
more. They presented Jesus as the non-apocalyptic Cynic based on recon-
structions of the Sayings Q Gospel[1] among other historical conclusions.

I learned about the fundamental issues in the field of New Testament
scholarship and the ongoing quest for the historical Jesus. However, I never
became a scholar in that field myself. I did pursue other fields in scholarship, earning a Ph.D. in linguistics in 2017. Therefore, I must confess that
this work is not a *scholarly* work as such, but produced by a scholar in a field
that is not my specialty. However, this is somewhat beyond the purpose of
this work. Let me explain.

---

1. A hypothetical, reconstructed document based on the commonalities between
Matthew and Luke against material not found in Mark.

As I embarked on a decades-long journey to uncover the mystery of the man behind Christianity, I went through several phases. First, I thought perhaps the Jesus Seminar was right. Perhaps he was a Cynic, a wisdom sage from Galilee. But that theory lost its hold on me, for a number of reasons. I considered other possibilities. Perhaps Jesus was an apocalyptic prophet, *à la* Bart Ehrman and countless others. This had a certain sway to it, but ultimately I was not fully convinced. Perhaps Jesus was who Christians say he was, a messianic claimant from the first century CE. For other reasons, that was not convincing either.

The more I searched, the more it felt like there was actually no answer. I considered that perhaps there was no historical Jesus. This is a conclusion called *mythicism*, which is not in vogue among biblical scholars, but has a certain following among non-orthodox scholars and former Christians. It seemed like the earliest memories from the Christian community were shrouded in mystery, perhaps so lost to history that they were now nothing more than myths.

However, I thought that it seemed unlikely that there was *no* historical memory among the countless stories of a man called Jesus. There had to be some historical kernel of truth at the bottom of it all. It was then that I started to consider the types of evidence that existed to make any substantial claims. Certainly there are some scattered non-Christian historical references from Greco-Roman authors, but these offer not much more than to say that those authors had heard that there was a man named "Christ" who founded a group called the "Christians." This was a common assumption in ancient times, that groups were normally named after someone. The Church Fathers thought that the Judeo-Christian sect, the Ebionites, was founded by a man named Ebion, when in reality it likely comes from the Hebrew *evyon*, "poor."

No, the Greco-Roman texts really only establish that there were *Christians* whenever the author was writing, at least by my reading. That conclusion brought me to the realization that there was really only one evidence for Jesus, that being the Christian record from the late first century CE and onward. This was the only material that existed to confirm or deny the existence of a historical Jesus of Nazareth. Or was it?

I returned to the question many years later, learning the Talmud as a Conservative Jew,[2] through the popular *Daf Yomi* program, in which par-

---

2. Here referring to the Jewish denomination in the United States, which stakes a middle ground between Orthodoxy and Reform Judaism, not a political ideology.

ticipants study a page of Talmud per day. I began to study passages about Jesus in the Talmud and sought further explanation about the meaning of these texts. I continued to think about these passages as I studied rabbinics later in life. It seemed that the question of Jesus in the Talmud needed a fresh look. I came to examine the issue as a linguist and student of rabbinics.

There is also an alternative tradition about Jesus, albeit no less biased than the Christian reading.[3] That is the Jewish tradition of Jesus the Nazarene, as he is referred to in the rabbinic tradition. Now, this account of Jesus' life is considered less reliable than the Christian sources, for a variety of reasons. However, I thought to myself, why should that be the case? There were two parties involved with the original Jesus story: the Jews who accepted him and his teachings and those who did not. Why should the plaintiff in this court case not be allowed to present its case?

---

3. The Talmud's account of Jesus' life is rejected for a number of reasons. It contradicts the Gospels on a number of occasions. These objections will be discussed later. Secondly, its late date is used as an objection to it having anything to say about the historical Jesus. For a variety of reasons, this is not a good reason to disregard the Talmud's account. In a number of cases, later sources are sometimes more trustworthy than older ones. For one such example, one can see E.P. Sanders' acceptance of the Johannine passion narrative over the Synoptics' accounts.

Acknowledgements

I WOULD LIKE TO EXPRESS gratitude to a number of people who made this project possible. First, and most importantly, to my wife for supporting my love of books and learning, which was the foundation of the learning that led to this book.

I'm grateful to a number of other friends who supported me along the way with encouraging remarks and listening to (sometimes brief) explanations of my work. I wanted to extend a special thank you to my rabbi, for dedicating a number of years to teaching me the intricacies of the Talmud.

I want to thank my editor, Dr. Amanda Haste, and a number of other friends at the National Coalition of Independent Scholars for their support and suggestions as I embarked on this journey. I also wish to express my gratitude to the team at Wipf and Stock for their guidance along the way.

Introduction

F OR A VARIETY OF reasons, the Talmudic account of Jesus' life has been ignored, most importantly by Jews, and for good reason. The Talmud has some rather unpleasant things to say about Jesus and that was something that could get you killed throughout most of Christian history. In countless instances the Talmudic account of Jesus was denied, censored, or shifted to another unknown person named "Yeshu"[1] who was *not* the Christian Jesus. This is a perfectly logical, rational, and justified approach when the result of such declarations is certain death. There is no reason to die to make a claim about Jesus.

This represents the rabbinic consensus of the majority of Jewish scholars today: that the accounts in the Talmud of a man named "Yeshu" are not references to the Christian Jesus but to another person from around the same time. Modern Jewish scholars try to read back into Jesus a certain type of Jewish orthodoxy. Perhaps he was a Pharisee, maybe he was of the House of Shammai, or perhaps an Essene; these are all conclusions reached by certain scholars in the ongoing Quest. The typical narrative is that Jesus was an observant Jew, who perhaps had some disagreements with the religious establishment of his time, but lived and died as a Jew in good standing. Then came Paul, who corrupted Jesus' Jewish teaching and invented Christianity as we know it.[2]

While there is some truth to the role of Paul in all of this, I would like to offer a counter-approach to this prevailing approach to Jesus by Jews

---

1. Jesus' name in the Talmud.

2. Robert Price explores this idea in his book, *Judaizing Jesus: How New Testament Scholars Created the Ecumenical Golem* (T & T Clark International).

which, if I may say so, also makes perfect sense. It comes from a spirit of ecumenism and tolerance that has never existed from the Christian side. Jewish leaders do not want to risk the possibility of losing that openness (and even friendship among certain Christian groups). Again, this is perfectly logical and rational. The spirit of freedom that Jews have been able to experience in the past two centuries is unique since pre-Christian times, and perhaps even throughout all history. However, there is an alternative tradition, seemingly maintained by Sephardic voices, given that they did not operate in a Christian society (except Sephardim in Europe and North America). Living in a Muslim society, where Christians were also minorities, gave these Jewish voices a chance to consider the Talmudic references in a different light.

A key point of departure between the rabbinic and Christian traditions about Yeshua is the dating of his life. Most notably, the rabbinic tradition places him some sixty years earlier, during the reign of King Jannaeus and as a disciple of Rabbi Yehoshua ben Peraḥyah. Jesus of Nazareth is assumed to have lived from around 6–4 BCE to around 30 CE. However, Jesus the Nazarene is assumed to have lived from around 100 BCE to around 66 BCE[3].

These chronologies are vastly different and imply a completely different context for the life and teaching of Jesus. However, it is true that even Christians were not entirely certain about the historical date of Jesus' existence. Epiphanius notes an alternative chronology for Jesus of Nazareth that matches with the chronology of Jesus the Nazarene.

> *Epiphanius, Panarion 29 5:1*
> The priesthood in the holy church is [actually] David's throne and kingly seat, for the Lord joined together and gave to his holy church both the kingly and high-priestly dignity, transferring to it the never-failing throne of David. For David's throne endured in line of succession until the time of Christ himself, rulers from Judah not failing until he came 'to whom the things kept in reserve belong, and he was the expectation of the nations.' With the advent of the Christ the rulers in line of succession from Judah, reigning until the time of Christ himself, ceased. For the line fell away and stopped from the time when he was born in Bethlehem of Judea under Alexander, who was of priestly and royal race. From Alexander onward this office ceased – from the days of Alexander

---

3. Putting his death after the reign of Alexander Jannaeus, during the reign of Aristobulus II. This precise dating is based on Abraham Ibn Daud's comments.

and Salina, who is also called Alexandra, to the days of Herod the king and Augustus the Roman emperor (Though this Alexander was crowned also, as one of the anointed priests and rulers.) For when the two tribes, the kingly and priestly, were united—- I mean the tribe of Judah with Aaron and the whole tribe of Levi—kings also became priests, for nothing hinted at in holy scripture can be wrong.) But then finally a gentile, King Herod, was crowned, and not David's descendants any more. But with the transfer of the royal throne the rank of king passed, in Christ, from the physical house of David and Israel to the church.

From the time that Augustus became Emperor [27 BCE] . . . until Judaea was made [entirely] subject and became tributary to them, its rulers having ceased from Judah, and Herod being appointed [as ruler] from the Gentiles [37 BCE], being a proselyte, however, and *Christ being born in Bethlehem of Judaea, and coming for the preaching [of the Gospel], the anointed rulers from Judah and Aaron having ceased, after continuing until the anointed ruler Alexander [76 BCE] and Salina, who was also Alexandra [67 BCE];* in which days the prophecy of Jacob was fulfilled: 'A ruler shall not cease from Judah and a leader from his thighs, until lie come for whom it is laid up, and he is the expectation of the nations'—that is, the Lord who was born. *Panarion*, Ch. 51 (emphasis added)[4]

4. The reference in Epiphanius is debated. Richard Carrier accepts this as referring to Judeo-Christian belief that Jesus lived in the first century BCE, while others do not. The context is a presentation of Nazoraean beliefs in Epiphanius' heresiological work, The *Panarion*. However, he digresses and discusses the names of early Christians, including the name "Jessaeans", supposedly originating from Jesse, the father of David, the ancient King of Israel. Epiphanius notes that the Davidic line and kingship is combined with the Aaronic priesthood in the Church, almost through a transferal of power, from the Davidic throne to the Church. This happened almost in succession, as the Davidic line continued from David himself until Christ. During Alexander's time (the Hasmonean dynasty), the priestly and kingly offices were combined and the Hasmoneans were not of Davidic descent. Epiphanius then states in 3:4 that this combined priest-king role died after Alexander, under Salina "known as Alexandra". The text is confusing because Epiphanius is grouping together a number of different rulers. After Alexander's death in 76 BCE, Salome Alexandra reigned from 76–67 BCE. There was considerable political instability after her, with Hyrcanus II (67–66 BCE), Aristobulus II (66–63 BCE) alternating, back to Hyrcanus II (63–40 BCE) and finally ending in Antigonus (40–37 BCE). Herod the Great finally reigned from 37–4 BCE. Epiphanius skips over thirty years of history to make his point about the end of the priest-king role. Epiphanius then states the Davidic line died with Herod's ascension to the throne, because Herod was a "gentile" and not part of the Davidic line. Jesus passes his Davidic and priestly (through the Order of Melchizedek) lineages to the Church. I read the passage as attacking his imagined interlocutors, the Judeo-Christians, who likely believed in literal interpretations of the messianic kingdom and dynastic succession.

Iraneus also proposes a different chronology for Jesus from an orthodox perspective. He argued that Jesus lived to be *fifty*, placing his death under Emperor Claudius (41–54 CE).

> *Irenaeus, Against Heresies 2.22:4–6*
>
> Being thirty years old when He came to be baptized, and then possessing the full age of a Master, He came to Jerusalem, so that He might be properly acknowledged by all as a Master. For He did not seem one thing while He was another, as those affirm who describe Him as being man only in appearance; but what He was, that He also appeared to be. Being a Master, therefore, He also possessed the age of a Master, not despising or evading any condition of humanity, nor setting aside in Himself that law which He had appointed for the human race, but sanctifying every age, by that period corresponding to it which belonged to Himself. For He came to save all through means of Himself—all, I say, who through Him are born again to God—infants, and children, and boys, and youths, and old men. He therefore passed through every age, becoming an infant for infants, thus sanctifying infants; a child for children, thus sanctifying those who are of this age, being at the same time made to them an example of piety, righteousness, and submission; a youth for youths, becoming an example to youths, and thus sanctifying them for the Lord. So likewise He was an old man for old men, that He might be a perfect Master for all, not merely as respects the setting forth of the truth, but also as regards age, sanctifying at the same time the aged also, and becoming an example to them likewise. Then, at last, He came on to death itself, that He might be *the first-born from the dead, that in all things He might have the pre-eminence,* (Colossians 1:18) the Prince of life, Acts 3:15 existing before all, and going before all.
>
> They, however, that they may establish their false opinion regarding that which is written, *to proclaim the acceptable year of the Lord,* maintain that He preached for one year only, and then suffered in the twelfth month. [In speaking thus,] they are forgetful to their own disadvantage, destroying His whole work, and robbing Him of that age which is both more necessary and more honorable than any other; that more advanced age, I mean, during which also as a teacher He excelled all others. For how could He have had disciples, if He did not teach? And how could He have taught, unless He had reached the age of a Master? For when He came to be baptized, He had not yet completed His thirtieth year, but was beginning to be about thirty years of age (for thus Luke, who has mentioned His years, has expressed it: *Now Jesus was, as*

it were, beginning to be thirty years old, (Luke 3:23) when He came to receive baptism); and, [according to these men,] He preached only one year reckoning from His baptism. On completing His thirtieth year He suffered, being in fact still a young man, and who had by no means attained to advanced age. Now, that the first stage of early life embraces thirty years, and that this extends onwards to the fortieth year, every one will admit; but from the fortieth and fiftieth year a man begins to decline towards old age, which our Lord possessed while He still fulfilled the office of a Teacher, even as the Gospel and all the elders testify; those who were conversant in Asia with John, the disciple of the Lord, [affirming] that John conveyed to them that information. And he remained among them up to the times of Trajan. Some of them, moreover, saw not only John, but the other apostles also, and heard the very same account from them, and bear testimony as to the [validity of] the statement. Whom then should we rather believe? Whether such men as these, or Ptolemæus, who never saw the apostles, and who never even in his dreams attained to the slightest trace of an apostle?

But, besides this, those very Jews who then disputed with the Lord Jesus Christ have most clearly indicated the same thing. For when the Lord said to them, *Your father Abraham rejoiced to see My day; and he saw it, and was glad,* they answered Him, *You are not yet fifty years old, and have You seen Abraham?* John 8:56–57 Now, such language is fittingly applied to one who has already passed the age of forty, without having as yet reached his fiftieth year, yet is not far from this latter period. But to one who is only thirty years old it would unquestionably be said, *You are not yet forty years old.* For those who wished to convict Him of falsehood would certainly not extend the number of His years far beyond the age which they saw He had attained; but they mentioned a period near His real age, whether they had truly ascertained this out of the entry in the public register, or simply made a conjecture from what they observed that He was above forty years old, and that He certainly was not one of only thirty years of age. For it is altogether unreasonable to suppose that they were mistaken by twenty years, when they wished to prove Him younger than the times of Abraham. For what they saw, that they also expressed; and He whom they beheld was not a mere phantasm, but an actual being of flesh and blood. He did not then want much of being fifty years old; and, in accordance with that fact, they said to Him, *You are not yet fifty years old, and have You seen Abraham?* He did not therefore preach only for one year, nor did He suffer in the twelfth

5

month of the year. For the period included between the thirtieth and the fiftieth year can never be regarded as *one* year, unless indeed, among their Æons, there be so long years assigned to those who sit in their ranks with Bythus in the Pleroma; of which beings Homer the poet, too, has spoken, doubtless being inspired by the Mother of their [system of] error

Abraham ibn Daud is one such Jewish figure who took the chronology in the Talmud seriously, as did Rabbi José Faur in his book, *The Gospel according to the Jews*, which reads more like a Jewish textual critique of the Gospels as we have them now. Both Sephardic figures are separated by around one thousand years.

Ibn Daud was a philosopher, historian, and astronomer, from Córdoba, Spain, born around the year 1110 CE and died around 1180 CE. His work, *Sefer Ha Qabbalah*, the Book of Tradition, is most important for our purposes: the Book of Tradition is a defense of Rabbinic Judaism against Karaite Judaism, a sect that denies the oral Torah of rabbinic Judaism. Ibn Daud is also noted for his Aristotelian philosophy, which influenced another famous Spanish Jew, Moses Maimonides, who became one of the world's most well-known Jewish philosophers, in addition to a number of Jewish theological and *halakhic* works.

Ibn Daud mentions Jesus in his Book of Traditions and presents the Talmudic chronology as authentic, noting that the Talmud *does* mention Jesus the Nazarene, the founder of Christianity, and that the Talmudic record is accurate.

> *Ibn Daud, The Book of Tradition, II.95—114, pp. 20–21*
>
> The historical works of the Jews state that this Joshua [Yehoshua] ben Peraḥyah was the teacher of Jesus the Nazarene. If this is so, it follows that he lived in the time of King Janneus. However, the historical works of the gentiles state that he was born in the days of Herod and crucified in the days of his son Archelaus. Now this is a significant difference of opinion, for there is a discrepancy between them of more than 110 years ... [The gentile historians] argue this point so vehemently in order to prove that the Temple and kingdom of Israel endured for but a short while after his crucifixion. However, we have it as an authentic tradition from the Mishnah and the Talmud, which did not distort anything, that Rabbi Joshua b. Perachiah fled to Egypt in the days of Alexander, that is, Janneus, and with him fled Jesus the Nazarene. We also have it as an authentic tradition that he was born in the fourth year of the reign of King Alexander, which was the year 263 after the

building of the Second Temple, and the fifty-first year of the reign of the Hasmonean dynasty. In the year 299 after the building of the Temple, he was apprehended at the age of thirty-six in the third year of the reign of Aristobulus the son of Janneus.

One can look to Yehudah HaLevi's *Kuzari* 3:65 or Maimonides' *Epistle to the Yemenites* or Abraham ibn Daud's *Sefer Ha-Qabbalah*, which presuppose historical validity to the Talmudic narrative.

José Faur was a Syrian Jew who was born in Argentina in 1934 and died in 2020. He was a professor at the Jewish Theological Seminary and the Spertus Institute for Jewish Learning and Leadership, as well as Bar Ilan University in Israel. He is noted for his preservation of classical Sephardic learning and defense of Maimonidean philosophy in Judaism. His book, *The Gospel According to the Jews*, is more akin to a critique of the Christian Scriptures from a Jewish perspective. Faur notes that his personal views about the historical Jesus are more in line with mainstream views that Jesus was a Jewish teacher of some sorts in the first century CE. Faur does not comment on the chronology of Jesus' life.

Prominent voices such as Naḥmanides have tried to distance the Talmudic narrative from the Jesus of Christianity to avoid the wrath of the Church. Others, such as Jacob Emden, have even tried to say positive things about the historical Jesus against Paul-as-founder-of-Christianity. Ashkenazi printings of the Talmud engaged in self-censorship, removing many of the negative things said about Jesus, to preserve the lives of the Jews in Europe. Several modern authors have commented on the historical validity of the Talmud's narrative. Earlier authors such as Pick's *Jesus in the Talmud* or Dalman's *Jesus Christ in the Talmud, Midrash, Zohar, and Liturgy of the Synagogue* ascribe minimalist historical validity, as do later authors such as Herford's *Christianity in the Talmud and Midrash*, Klausner's *Jesus of Nazareth: His Life, Times, and Teaching* or Lauterbach's *Jesus in the Talmud*, which found little or some value in the Talmud's validity as a historical source. Other authors such as Van Voorst in his *Jesus Outside the New Testament* have used the Talmud in some ways in their conclusions about the historical Jesus. Most notably, the Talmud provides an independent, opposition and alternative view to the Christian narrative. Peter Schafer reads the narrative in a similar light, as a Jewish *response* to Christianity. Johann Maier, John Meier, and Jacob Neusner do not believe the Talmud has any historical memories of Jesus.

René Salm is a modern author who accepts the Talmudic accounts as providing insight into the historical Jesus. Salm sees Yeshua ben Pantera as the true founder of Christianity and with the development of Pauline Christianity as the nucleus of later proto-orthodoxy. Several of Salm's assertions formed this reading of Talmudic and Christian sources. He notes the importance of pre-Christian Gnosticism in the development of Christianity, noting that Gnosticism was fairly widespread throughout pre-Christian times. It was found in the archeological record from ancient times, and even with some possible references in the Hebrew Scriptures.[5] He adds some interesting assertions that should be included in our discussion of the historical Jesus. Salm notes that there are no historical sources, besides Christian texts, that corroborate the existence of Jesus (besides the Talmudic record) and points out that many New Testament texts might include interpolations.[6] In a similar vein, Salm reiterates that the Apostle Paul did not have any connection to the historical Jesus, because Paul's descriptions of Jesus are entirely spiritual and he even claims that his gospel does not come from men but from the heavenly Christ.[7] This is evident in Paul's writings, as there are little to no references to any historical details about Jesus' life and only traces of his teaching. The New Testament shows a developing Christology, doctrine of Christ, from a purely spiritual Jesus to the fusion of the divine Christ with an earthly man.[8] The theology of the Gospels, particularly Mark, is more accurately called docetism, where the spiritual Jesus/Christ came down and indwelled a body on earth, the historical man, that is "Jesus" was a purely spiritual phenomenon to the Pauline communities and represented the spiritual aspect of a saved person.[9] Salm posits that Jesus the Nazarene of the first century BCE was the founder of Christianity[10], concurring with the view of Alvar Ellegard.[11] The Gospels invent a different historical character at a later date, which contain some memories of the historical Jesus the Nazarene, who lived much earlier.[12]

---

5. Salm, R. *NazarethGate*, pp. 406–408.

6. Salm, R. *NazarethGate*, pp. 402–406.

7. Salm, R. *NazarethGate*, pp. 408–411

8. Salm, R. *NazarethGate*, pp. 412–417.

9. Salm, R. *NazarethGate*, pp. 417–418.

10. Salm, R. *NazarethGate*, pp. 419–471.

11. Ellegard, Alvar. *Jesus*.

12. Ellegard thinks that Jesus is the Christian name for the earlier Essene Teacher of Righteousness, who lived in the second century BCE.

Of course, the rabbinic traditions are inherently biased, but no more so than the Christian tradition, which *is the only alternative*. There are no historical sources that provide an independent narrative—only sources that confirm that there might have been a historical man named Jesus. To be fair, there is another alternative, that of the Gnostic Gospels, but, if what I present is true, then this is the same as the rabbinic tradition.

My quest was to take these sources seriously, at least as a thought experiment, to contrast the narratives of Jesus' life as found in the Gospels, particularly Mark, and the rabbinic sources in the Talmud as well as certain other references).

First, we must consider the Talmud as a historical source, for it is a complicated documentary source.

USING THE TALMUD AS A HISTORICAL SOURCE

The Talmud is primarily not a historical document. Instead it is a collection of legal records of the rabbinic circles in Palestine and Babylonia, each compiled into different legal collections. The Talmud contains two documents: the Mishnah and the Gemara. These are not presented as separate works but woven together because they are intertextual. The Mishnah is viewed as a standardized version of the Oral Torah, stemming from traditional Judaism's belief that God revealed the Torah in two forms to Moses on Mount Sinai, in both a written and oral form. The written Torah is the Five Books of Moses as contained in Jewish (and Christian) Bibles today, whereas the latter was believed by the Pharisees and Rabbis to be transmitted orally:

> *Pirke Avot 1:1*[13]
> Moses received the Torah at Sinai and transmitted it to Joshua, Joshua to the elders, and the elders to the prophets, and the prophets to the Men of the Great Assembly.[14]

13. The Mishnah and Tosefta are generally referenced by chapter and verse number (Sanhedrin 10:2), like Scriptural references. The Talmud is referenced by page number (folio) with the letters *a* and *b* denoting the side of the page (Berakhot 13b). The Jerusalem Talmud can be referenced by page number, with accompanying page side references, or by chapter and verse (Jerusalem Demai 2b; Jerusalem Sotah 1:1). Wherever the word "Talmud" appears without modifiers, the Babylonian Talmud is being referenced. The Jerusalem Talmud is always referred to with the modifier "Jerusalem".

14. All citations from rabbinic texts are taken from sefaria.org with parenthetical commentary from Rabbi Adin Steinsaltz removed. However, his comments that aid in understanding the text are left in. Readers can check against the text on Sefaria to see the

The Great Assembly transmitted this oral Torah to the *"zugot"*, pairs of scholars who taught together in the second and first century BCE. The chain of transmission passed to the Rabbis, who became the guardians of this tradition. After the destruction of the Temple and Bar Kokhba revolt, the oral Torah was recorded in writing, traditionally ascribed to Yehudah Ha Nasi (the Prince, a recognized position of leadership among Jews). This became the Mishnah. This is a different kind of text to earlier Jewish literature[15] which presents legal decisions or debates about legal decisions without arriving at a conclusion.

The Mishnah was studied in rabbinic *yeshivot* (legal schools) in both Palestine and Babylon for the next few centuries.[16] Eventually, another work was published to supplement the Mishnah, which became the Talmud. The Talmud includes most of the Mishnah and the Gemara, often called a commentary. However, it is better understood as a compilation of legal records, because the Rabbis acted as scholars and lawyers for their communities. The Gemara tries to clarify the statements in the Mishnah, arrive at legal decisions, or provide a Scriptural basis for rabbinic decisions, creating a sort of Jewish rhetoric that links thought to the biblical text. The Gemara often presents legal statements, called *baraita (pl. baraitot)* which are traditions attributed to the Rabbis of earlier eras but which were not recorded in the Mishnah.

The Talmud is a complex document, or rather, a library, consisting of 63 tractates or volumes and 2,711 double-sided folios. The Talmud contains two works within it. First, the Mishnah, as we have seen above, is a standardized text of the Oral Law or Oral Torah, an unwritten explanation of the meaning of the written Torah, believed to be given at the same time as the written Torah at Sinai. These ideas were transmitted orally for some time before their composition in the Mishnah in the second century CE, but it is hard to know exactly how long this process continued. The impetus for the writing of the Mishnah was the destruction of the Second Temple and subsequent war under the messianic claimant, Bar Kokhba. It seems that the Rabbis were worried about losing the bulk of their oral tradition and set out to write the Mishnah. It was compiled by Judah Ha Nasi, often

---

original Talmudic text.

15. Neusner, *The Mishnah.*

16. See, Faur, *Horizontal Society,* for a Sephardic approach to understanding the development of the Talmud. Saiman, *Halakhah* and Freedman, *The Talmud,* present Ashkenazi understanding of its development.

simply referred to as "Rabbi" in the text. The Mishnah became the most important document studied in the various *yeshivot* throughout the Jewish world in Israel and Babylon.

As time progressed, the political situation of the Jews did not improve and it became necessary to record further oral traditions. These further written compilations became what is known today as the Talmud. There are actually two Talmuds, one from the Land of Israel (called the Jerusalem Talmud) and one from the diaspora community in Babylon (called the Babylonian Talmud).

What is the Talmud? This is a crucial thing to understand if one is to use the Talmud as any sort of source. It is a compilation of the records of the *yeshivot* in Galilee and Babylon. The *yeshivot* somewhat resembled both a college and a court.[17] The rabbis sat together to learn the written Torah (five books of Moses) and the oral Torah (the Mishnah). Their discussions and decisions were recorded in the Talmuds. The "commentary" (as it is often incorrectly called) of the Mishnah is called the Gemara, from the Aramaic root meaning "to complete." The Gemara often seeks to clarify the language of a Mishnah, to establish a connection with a biblical verse (often called a "source" but more like a way of connecting the ideas via rhetoric) or provide additional statements to support an idea. These additional statements are called *baraita* (pl. *Baraitot*, from the Aramaic, "outside"), which are traditions from the tannaitic period that are not included in the Mishnah or Tosefta.[18]

The Talmuds are concerned with *precise* language and present baraitot with a technical phrase, *tannu rabbanan*, "the rabbis taught."[19] This introduces a *baraita* "on the record" i.e. into the official Jewish legal record in the Talmud. There are statements of lesser authoritative status, which are introduced with other linguistic phrasing. Sometimes there are discussions about topics related to the Mishnah that are used to arrive at a legal conclusion (*halakhah*) such as stories that demonstrate the point a *mishnah* is making. It is thus important to understand what sort of document the Talmud is, when embarking on a quest to use it as a source for the historical

---

17. This description is based on the Talmudic record.

18. Hauptman, Judith. *Re-Reading the Mishnah*, proposes that the Tosefta is the earlier collection and comments on an early "ur-Mishnah" that preceded both the Tosefta and the current copy of the Mishnah.

19. Faur, José. *The Horizontal Society*.

Jesus. I think it is often the case that people researching the historical Jesus do not truly understand the Talmud or how it functions.

That being the case, I think it will be beneficial to show a piece of the first Mishnah, about the recitation of the Shema in the evening and related Gemara, in order for the reader to understand what type of text we are dealing with here. The text presents *both* the translated text and commentary to aid in understanding. The pure translation is recorded in **bold**, whereas explanation is presented in regular text.

The very first Mishnah describes the time frame within which the text of the Shema must be recited. There are a few statements given to establish the legal positions available at the time, and the Gemara begins by asking why the Mishnah begins with the evening Shema before the morning Shema.

> *Babylonian Talmud Berakhot 2a*
>
> **MISHNA: From when,** that is, from what time, does **one recite** Shema **in the evening? From the time when the priests enter to partake of their** teruma. Until when does the time for the recitation of the evening *Shema* extend? **Until the end of the first watch.** The term used in the Torah (Deuteronomy 6:7) to indicate the time for the recitation of the evening *Shema* is *beshokhbekha*, when you lie down, which refers to the time in which individuals go to sleep. Therefore, the time for the recitation of *Shema* is the first portion of the night, when individuals typically prepare for sleep. **That is the statement of Rabbi Eliezer.**
>
> **GEMARA:** The Mishna opens with the laws concerning the appropriate time to recite *Shema* with the question: From when does one recite *Shema* in the evening? With regard to this question, the Gemara asks: **On the basis of what** prior knowledge **does** the tanna of our mishna ask: **From when?** It would seem from his question that the obligation to recite *Shema* in the evening was already established, and that the *tanna* seeks only to clarify details that relate to it. But our mishna is the very first mishna in the Talmud. The Gemara asks: **And furthermore, what distinguishes the evening** *Shema*, that it was taught **first? Let** the *tanna* **teach** regarding the recitation of **the morning** *Shema* **first.**

This brief text shows the type of discussion that can take place within the Talmud, and I will try to connect the text of the Gemara to the legal question in the Mishnah, as the discussion in the Gemara is always (somehow) tied to the original question.

Elman[20] points out that, due to the "pervasive orality" of Sassanid Persia, perhaps as much as two thirds of the Babylonian Talmud was orally transmitted and composed. The orality of Jewish Babylonian culture must be taken seriously, as is the bias for textual evidence in Western academia. Patterson[21], writing about music history, notes the false dichotomy between oral and written transmission, with an "imperfect" oral transmission and "perfect" literary transmission, dominant in Western thinking about textuality and orality. There is often a transferal from oral to textual, but this is seldom haphazard. The Talmud can be thought of as containing both *oral histories* and *oral traditions*, now transferred to writing.

There was a difference between Greco-Roman and Sasanian cultures vis-a-vis orality which is noted in the Jerusalem vs. Babylonian Jewish traditions. The Rabbis demonstrated a commitment to orality, prohibiting the written transmission of oral texts, even though this was eventually broken (Gittin 60a). While the Rabbis were able to write (Hullin 9a), few legal texts are described as existing in writing.[22] Few Sages are described as "scribes" who wrote legal documents in Babylon, in contrast to several Palestinian Sages described as Sages. The pervasive orality postdated the Talmudic period, continuing into Geonic times, as a tenth-century rabbi, Aaron Hacohen Sargado notes: "Our whole yeshiva, of which it is known that its version [of the Talmud] is from the mouths of the great ones, and most of them [i.e, the members of the yeshiva] do not know anything of a book."

Oral histories are "reminiscences, hearsay, or eyewitness accounts about events and situations which are contemporary, that is, which occurred during the lifetime of the informants" whereas oral traditions are "no longer contemporary. They have passed from mouth to mouth, for a period beyond the lifetime of the informants ... [they can be] spoken, sung, or called out on musical instruments only."[23] We expect oral tradition to make use of mnemonic devices, such as alliteration, repetition, assonance, and proverbial sayings to enhance memory. For this reason, there are some 16,000 acronyms in the Babylonian Talmud.[24]

It is hard to know exactly how much of the rabbinic record is historical and how much is an aspirational view of history, i.e. this is how

20. Elman, Yaakov. "Orality".
21. Patterson, Emma E. "Oral Transmission." p. 37
22. Elman, Yaakov. "Orality", p. 55–7.
23. Vansina, Jan. "Oral Tradition", pp. 11–12.
24. Elman, Yaakov. "Orality", p. 69

things *should have been*. There is an analogy to the biblical text itself here, considering the Deuteronomistic view of history as contrasted with the archaeological record. Certainly, there are episodes of historical insight in the Hebrew Bible, but these are skewed through a theological view of the world and its workings that must be taken into account.

Using the Talmud as a historical source can be problematic. There is a division of opinion on its worth as a historical source. Jacob Neusner views the Talmud as simply providing historical insight into the Jewish community that composed the document. Kraemer proposes a methodology to validate the historical reliability of the Talmud's record of history by relying on Neusner's proposed methodology. First, commonly attested traditions in both the Palestinian and Babylonian Talmud can be regarded as reflecting the original sages (rabbis) with whom they are associated. Secondly, some literary characteristics of texts in the Babylonian Talmud presume that they were written shortly after when the events described had actually occurred. Oppenheimer proposes a way to examine the historical validity of the Talmud, "My approach is a more systematic, combined examination of Talmudic sources in which they are read in relation to external, independent sources (when they are available), such as the writings of Roman historians, church fathers, and Persian authors, as well as the archaeological material, notably epigraphic material."[25]

Therefore, we can trust multiple attested traditions *more* than those with only one source within Rabbinic literature. It is likely, however, that traditions with only one source can tell us something about either the Rabbis themselves or the Christian communities they interacted with in the time period. For example, the Talmud contains a cryptic reference to Jesus by the name *Ben Stada*, which turns out to be a nickname, because Jesus' mother, Miriam, "strayed" from her husband and had a lover. This is a later Rabbinic tradition, from the Babylonian period, perhaps around 500 CE, although it is harder to date. This contrasts with more neutral discussion of Jesus' parentage in earlier sources from the second and third centuries CE. It is more likely that the earlier traditions preserve some historical memory over the later traditions. However, the later traditions are not entirely "useless" as historical records. These show us that the belief in the virgin birth had circulated among more groups by the time the Rabbis in Babylon were compiling their Talmud, and tells us how the Rabbis reacted to the idea of

25. Oppenheimer, Aharon. "Talmudic Literature," p. 17.

Jesus' virgin birth. This is one example of how later, less attested traditions can help us understand the context of either the Rabbis or the Christians.

This book is a thought experiment of sorts. Given that the historical record for Jesus' existence is debated, beyond the pages of the New Testament, it seems that we are left with two traditions: the Christian tradition and the Jewish tradition. Most Christian accounts (even Gnostic) use the Gospel of Mark as a starting point to discuss Jesus' life and add their own unique flavor to the account (except the Gospel of Thomas). My argument in this book is that the Rabbis *did* have a unified and coherent vision of who Jesus was and why they did not accept him as part of their circle. That is to say that Yeshu *is* Jesus (and Ben Stada is Yeshu). With the assertion that the Rabbis had a coherent vision of who Jesus was, we can compile the references to Jesus in the Talmud and construct this vision. What was Jesus' name? Who were his parents? What kind of Jew was he? Did he have a teacher? What did *he* teach? Did he perform miracles? And, why was he executed?

This is the story I want to tell in this book, by using the Talmud's accounts and relevant historical records to show who Jesus was, according to the Rabbis.[26]

---

26. Throughout the text, I use the name "Jesus of Nazareth" to refer to the Christian account of Jesus and "Jesus the Nazarene" to refer to the Jewish account.

A Hasmonean Context for Jesus

ASSUMING A HASMONEAN CONTEXT for the life of Jesus changes our perception of him and his movement. The Gospels were written with the occupation of Palestine by Rome in mind; whether to assuage that problem, or to show the valiant efforts of Jesus against the Romans, is up for debate. The presence of Rome is felt throughout the Gospels, even where it seems that the Gospels are purposefully *deleting* references to Rome.

However, if the Talmud's chronology is correct, that would not be the case. Jesus would have lived under *Jewish* rulers in the Hasmonean dynasty, the Jewish ruling class from 140 to 37 BCE. The dynasty was established by Simon Thassi, the second son of the Maccabees, after the successful revolt against the Seleucid Empire from 167 to 141 BCE. The Maccabean Revolt was an uprising against the policies of Antiochus IV who oppressed Jewish religious practice when he sacked Jerusalem. The simultaneous attacks of the Roman Republic and Parthian Empire against the Seleucids allowed the Jews to restore political autonomy under the Hasmoneans.

The Maccabees were a group opposed to the Hellenistic practices and regulation of the Seleucids. This was the practice of Greek culture by Jews, some of whom participated willingly, while others were prohibited from traditional, Judean practices. The construction of gymnasiums and other institutions of Greek cities was common during this time, as was the avoidance of traditional Jewish ritual, such as circumcision. The Maccabees were a priestly family, who led the revolt against the Seleucids. The climax of their revolt was the restoration of Jewish worship in the Temple in Jerusalem, resulting in the religious observance of Hanukkah.

The Maccabees allied with the Roman Republic to rid Palestine of the Greeks. The Maccabees benefited from internal conflict among the Seleucids, which helped them fulfill their goal of political independence. However, after allying with the Romans in 161 BCE, the Jews would have to live under Seleucid rule for some time, until Simon assumed the leadership of the people in 141 BCE.

Simon was assassinated in 135 BCE along with his brothers Matthias and Judah, and that year John Hyrcanus became the king. The Hasmoneans reigned semi-autonomously in the earlier days, under the indirect rule of the Seleucid Empire. Hyrcanus began to expand his political influence in the region, conquering areas around Judea, including Idumea, and forcing the Idumeans to convert to Judaism. After his death, Hyrcanus' son Aristobulus forcibly took the throne from his mother, who was designated to succeed her husband, and became the first Hasomean to take the title "king" (*basileus*), becoming Aristobulus I in 104 BCE.

Aristobulus died painfully in 103 BCE after only one year of kingship. He was succeeded by Alexander Jannaeus who reigned from 103 to 76 BCE. During his reign there was a civil war among the Jews and the kingdom lost many of the conquests of his predecessors. Alexander Jannaeus fought with the Pharisees, who opposed him being the king and priest, in addition to the forced conversion of the Idumeans. At that time, the Pharisees and Sadducees were more like political parties, and Alexander led a brutal opposition and persecution of the Pharisees.

According to the Talmud, this is the time that Jesus is said to have lived. Jesus was born under the reign of Alexander Jannaeus and died under either the reign of Hyrcanus II or Aristobulus II. He fled to Egypt with Yehoshua ben Peraḥyah when Alexander began his campaign against the Pharisees. After Jesus' death, the Hasmonean dynasty began to decline, becoming a Roman client state in 63 BCE, when the Roman Republic invaded the area. It was eventually replaced by the Herodian dynasty in 37 BCE. Alexander's rule passed to his wife, Salome, who reigned as the regent, while his son, Hyrcanus II, held the office of high priest. A civil war arose between Hyrcanus II and his brother Aristobulus II who wanted the throne. Eventually, Hyrcanus II lost and renounced the kingship, accepting only the office of high priest.

After this point in history, the story of the Hasmoneans becomes even more complicated, and beyond the scope of what interests us now. However, what is important to know is that the Hasmoneans were a corrupt ruling class that were often involved with conflict, and who caused immense internal strife for the Jewish People. Their victory under the hands of the Maccabees led directly to the Roman occupation later in the first century BCE. Jesus lived during the time when the Hasmonean dynasty was beginning to wane. He lived in a time of civil war and persecution for his tribe, the Pharisees, and the bloodshed and brutality that he witnessed was the reason he left Palestine for Egypt.[1]

1. This is a very brief summary of the Hasmonean period. For a fuller account see Shaye Cohen, *From the Maccabees to the Mishnah* (Westminster John Knox Press).

What Was Jesus' Name?

I T SEEMS LIKE A basic question, but the details of Jesus' life are so obscured that we do not truly know his name. We have the common description, Jesus of Nazareth, used in Christian and some scholarly circles, and the Jewish description, Jesus the Nazarene. The latter part differs, reflecting divergent views on his origin and birthplace, but they agree on the first part: *Jesus*. However, this is a Greek name and Jesus was an Aramaic-speaking Jew from Palestine, so we may ask: what was his Aramaic or Hebrew name?

The name is typically translated as *Yeshua*, but in Jewish texts we see a variant *Yeshu*. So, which is it?

His was a common name, even being related to his teacher's name, as both *Yeshua* and *Yehoshua* are derived from the same root. It seems that the alternative, *Yeshu*, is nothing more than a difference in pronunciation; it is noted in the Talmud that the Galileans did not pronounce the *ayin* as distinct from the *alef* (Eruvin 53b)[1]. The *ayin* was a guttural sound not found in English, but common in Arabic. *Alef* originally did have a sound but had lost that sound over time. This refutes another common point about the name "Yeshu," that it is an acronym for "may his name be blotted out" in Hebrew. It seems more likely that his name would be *Yeshu'a* with the final *ayin* of his name being omitted.

---

1. In typical reconstructed phonologies of rabbinic Hebrew, the *alef* was pronounced like a glottal stop (the sound made between the vowels when pronouncing the English *uh-oh* or in certain dialects in England when pronouncing the letter *t* the word *bottle*. The *ayin* was pronounced as a voiced pharyngeal approximant, a sound that does not exist in English, but which is equivalent to the Arabic sound of the same name.

Even Jastrow's dictionary of the Aramaic of the Talmud and other Rabbinic literature notes that Yeshu is a variant of Yeshua.

Jastrow

יֵשׁוּ (abbrev. of יֵשׁוּעַ) pr. n. m. *Jesus* of Nazareth. Snh. 43ª י׳ הנוצרי Ms. M. (ed. only י׳). Ib. 107ᵇ (represented as a disciple of Rabbi Joshua b. Peraḥyah, with whom he fled to Egypt); Sot. 47ª. Ab. Zar. 17ª מצאתי אדם אחד מתלמידי י׳ הנוצרי ויעקב וכ׳ I met one of the disciples of J. the Nazarean whose name was Jacob (v. יַעֲקֹב 5); Tosef. Ḥull. II, 24 יֵשׁוּעַ בן פנטירי (Var. פנטרי); Ib. 22 ובא . . . ישוע בן פנטרא and Jacob . . . came to cure him with the name of J. the son of Pantera; Ab. Zar. 27ᵇ (v. Rabb. D. S. a. l. note 300); Y. ib. II, 40ᵈ bot. נימא לך בשם י׳ בן פנדרא shall I speak a charm to thee in the name of J. the son of Pandera; Y. Sabb. XIV, 14ᵈ bot. משם ולחש ליה משמיה די׳ פ׳ . . . Ib. של ישו פנדירא and he whispered to him a charm, in behalf of J. P.; [In Babli editions published unter censorial restrictions all the above quoted passages are omitted or changed; in Koh. R. to I, 8 פלני is substituted.]

Jesus' name is found in earlier sources, such as Tosefta Ḥullin 2, which contains two explicit references to Jesus, or Yeshu[a] ben Pandira/Pantiri, as he is called there. These are semi-polemical stories but stated matter-of-factly, not with any intended puns or obfuscation, like the stories of Ben Stada or the later *Toledot Yeshu* narrative. There are two narratives about Jesus in this portion of the Tosefta, and both are referenced in other places in rabbinic literature. However, because these are the earliest versions of each story, I will discuss them here, with some reference to any changes in the later versions.

Tosefta, Ḥullin 2.20–24

Flesh which is found in the hand of a Gentile is allowed for use; in the hand of a heretic it is forbidden for use. That which comes from a house of idolatry, lo, this is the flesh of sacrifices of the dead, because they say, "Slaughtering by a heretic is idolatry, their bread is Samaritan bread, their wine is wine offered, their fruits are not tithed, their books are books of witchcraft, and their sons are bastards." One does not sell to them or receive from them, or take from them or give to them; one does not teach their sons trades, and one does not obtain healing from them, either healing of property or healing of life. The case of Rabbi Eliazar ben Damah, whom a serpent bit. There came in Jacob, a man of Chephar Sama, to cure him in the name of *Yeshua ben Pandira*, but Rabbi Ishmael did not allow it. He said, "You are not permitted, ben Damah."

He said, "I will bring you a proof that he may heal me." But he had not finished bringing a proof when he died. Rabbi Ishmael said, "Happy you are, ben Damah, for you have departed in peace and have not broken through the ordinances of the wise; for upon every one who breaks through the fence of the wise, punishment comes at last, as it is written, 'Whosoever breaks a fence, a serpent shall bite him' (= Ecclesiastes 10:8)." (also in Jerusalem Talmud, *Avodah Zara* 2: 2)

This first story establishes the name of our character, *Yeshua ben Pandira*. I believe that *Pantera* is the best vocalization of the name, because it is preserved in the archaeological record[2]:

Corpus Inscriptionum Latinarum 3.7514 (Bingerbrück, Germany, AD 31–52): Tiberius Iulius Abdes Pantera of Sidon, 62 years old, soldier of 40 yearly stipends, former standard bearer for the first cohort of archers, lies here.

One must read the story in its legal context, which is a presentation of the relationships between Jews and Gentiles. The story is presented as evidence for the *halakhic* view of Rabbi Ishmael. This text presents important information about the association of Jesus with magic, in this case magical incantations meant to provide healing, a theme which we will cover in depth later. It does not tell us much about the man, Yeshua himself. Rabbi Eliazar ben Damah is an interesting character himself. He is little known throughout Rabbinic literature and is only called a rabbi here in the Tosefta. He has another moment with Rabbi Ishmael (whose teachings are better preserved):

Menaḥot 99b
Ben Dama, son of Rabbi Yishmael's sister, asked Rabbi Yishmael: In the case of one **such as I, who has learned the entire Torah, what is the** *halakha* **with regard to studying Greek wisdom?** Rabbi Yishmael **recited this verse about him: "This Torah scroll shall not depart from your mouth, and you shall contemplate in it day and night." Go and search for an hour that is neither** part **of the day nor** part **of the night, and learn Greek wisdom in it.**

These two texts link Rabbi Eliazar ben Damah with both Hellenism and Christianity, neither of which were appreciated by the Rabbis. A full discussion of this Talmudic passage is beyond the scope of our aims here;

2. Tabor, *Jesus Dynasty,* p. 65..

however, Ben Dama's openness to Jacob's magical incantations at the end of his life also tell of his openness to magic itself. To cure or heal "in the name of" someone was common in Jewish magical traditions.[3] Jesus' own teacher in the rabbinic tradition, Yehoshua ben Peraḥyah, is also associated with incantation bowls in the magical tradition. The disciples in the Gospels even reference casting out demons in Jesus' name, "Lord, even the demons are subject to us in your name!" (Luke 10:17).

My suspicion is that the Tannaim, in particular, were uncomfortable with the magical and Gnostic traditions (perhaps for rational and good reason) and sought to defend their understanding of Judaism over any remaining competition after the Destruction of the Temple and subsequent disappearance of other major Jewish sects. There is a gradual hardening towards magic, Gnosticism Judeo-Christianity and Samaritanism[4] from the composition of the Mishnah to the composition of the Talmuds.

Another rabbi who had a run-in with the early Jewish Christians was Rabbi Eliezer. The second half of the text in Tosefta mentions the arrest of Rabbi Eliezer, who also came into conflict with the Sages in other incidents and was excommunicated for going against the majority ruling with regards to the ritual impurity of a certain type of oven.

Here, Rabbi Eliezer was arrested for heresy (for which he was acquitted). Rabbi Akiva came to comfort his teacher after the trial, but Rabbi Eliezer did not want to be comforted because he was distraught by being associated with heresy. He then recalled an incident with the same Jacob, a famous Christian healer.

> The case of R. Eliezer, who was arrested for heretics, and they brought him to the tribunal for judgment. The governor said to him, "Does an old man like you occupy himself with such things?" He said to him, "Faithful is the Judge concerning me." The governor supposed that he only said this of him, but he was not thinking of any but his Father who is in Heaven. He said to him, "Since I am trusted concerning yourself, thus also I will be. I said, 'Perhaps these societies err concerning these things.' *Dimissus*, behold, you are released." And when he had been released from the tribunal, he was troubled because he had been arrested for heresy. His disciples came in to console him, but he would not take comfort. Rabbi

---

3. Alexander, "Incantations and Books of Magic."

4. For example, in earlier sources, the Samaritans are trusted on certain matters in Jewish law. However, by the time of the redaction of the Talmuds, the Samaritans are counted as non-Jews by the Rabbis.

Aqiba came in and said to him, "Rabbi, shall I say to you why you are perhaps grieving?" He said to him, "Say on." He said to him, "Perhaps one of the heretics has said to you a word of heresy and it has pleased you." He said, "By Heaven, you have reminded me! Once I was walking along the street of Sepphoris, and I met *Jacob of Kefar Sichnin* and he said to me a word of heresy in the name of *Yeshu ben Pantiri*, and it pleased me. And I was arrested for words of heresy because I transgressed the words of Torah, 'Keep your way far from her, and come not nigh the door of her house' (Proverbs 5:8), for 'she has cast down many wounded' (Proverbs 7:26)." And R. Eliezer used to say, "Ever let a man flee from what is hateful, and from that which resembles what is hateful."

I will not focus on the content of the teaching that Jacob presented to him, which is expanded in further detail in later Talmudic texts, but rather that what these two texts do reveal is that Jesus' name was *Yeshua ben Pantera*. The nature of each text here is not provocative but only meant to mention the name of the healer or heretic being referenced. This is important because we will later establish that Yeshua ben Pantera is the same as Yeshu HaNotsri and Ben Stada, as well as other equivalents. These texts also reveal that Jesus or Yeshu was associated with magical healing at the time of the various incidents recorded, which seems to be in the late first to early second century CE. There was also some oral teaching being preserved among his followers. Jacob, or Ya'akov, is mentioned several times in the Talmud, usually in connection with his healing in the name of Yeshu[a] ben Pantera. He also interacts with the Rabbis in other occasions, such as when he asked a theological question of Rabbi Yehudah Ha Nasi (the compiler of the Mishnah).

The earlier Jerusalem Talmud also contains a healing story with reference to Jesus' actual name. The grandson of Rabbi Joshua ben Levi, who was an active rabbi in the first half of the second century CE in the city of Lod in central Israel, suffered from choking.[5] A Christian comes to heal his grandson in the name of *Yeshua ben Pantera*. Rabbi Joshua asks what words he had spoken (which are not recorded) and declares that it would have been better for his grandson to die than to hear the Christian's words of heresy. Later, his grandson died. This text shows again that Jesus was known by the name *Yeshua ben Pantera* and that his name was used in connection with healing by later Nazarenes/Christians, perhaps using magical

---

5. Lod is about nine miles southeast of modern Tel Aviv.

incantation bowls. In the rabbinic record the association of Christians with healing is quite strong.

> *Jerusalem Talmud, Shabbat 14:4*
> His [Rabbi Yehoshua ben Levi] grandson suffered from choking; there came one, whispered something in the name of Jesus ben Pantera and he could breathe. When he left, he asked him what did you say over him? He answered, such and such words. He said, it would have been better for him had he died and not heard these words. It happened to him.

Certain other texts in the Mishnah[6] are regarded as possible indirect references to Yeshu[a] ben Pantera, but I do not find them convincing. I believe these tannaitic references in the Tosefta to be the earliest in the rabbinic record.

Non-Christian or non-Jewish references to Jesus are scant, but one of the more famous references is found in Josephus. However, this, or at least most of it, seems to be an obvious Christian interpolation and, at best, shows us that his name was *Iesous* in Greek. Most scholars agree that it is at least partially an interpolated text, meaning that some Christian scribes inserted parts or all of it. Even if it were authentic, I read it as demonstrating how Josephus understood Christian beliefs, rather than as a statement of who Jesus was. A good analogy would be how I, a non-Mormon, would relate the story of Joseph Smith. I know mostly what the Church of Jesus of the Latter-Day Saints (LDS) *claims* about Joseph Smith: he was a prophet who found golden tablets and translated them through the help of God, and the Book of Mormon is another testament of Jesus. I do not believe any of those statements to be true, but it is a historical fact that *Mormons* believe that.

> *Flavius Josephus: Antiquities of the Jews, Book 18, Chapter 3:3*
> About this time there lived Jesus, a wise man, if indeed one ought to call him a man. For he was one who performed surprising deeds and was a teacher of such people as accept the truth

---

6. *Mishnah, Yevamot 4:13* Which [forbidden offspring] is a *mamzer*? Any next of kin that is subject to a Torah prohibition that he should not engage in sexual relations with them; this is the statement of Rabbi Akiva. Shimon HaTimni says: any forbidden relation for which one is liable to receive *karet* at the hand of Heaven. And the *halakha* is in accordance with his statement. Rabbi Yehoshua says: any forbidden relation for which one is liable to receive court-imposed capital punishment. Rabbi Shimon ben Azzai said: I found a scroll recording people's lineages in Jerusalem, and it was written in it that so-and-so is a *mamzer* from an adulterous union with a married woman

gladly. He won over many Jews and many of the Greeks. He was the Christ. And when, upon the accusation of the principal men among us, Pilate had condemned him to a cross, those who had first come to love him did not cease. He appeared to them spending a third day restored to life, for the prophets of God had foretold these things and a thousand other marvels about him. And the tribe of the Christians, so called after him, has still to this day not disappeared.

Josephus' reference to Jacob (James) the "brother of Jesus, who was called the Christ" is perhaps more authentic. However, not all scholars agree and some think this is also an interpolation. This historical record only serves to confirm *Iesous* as the name of Jesus in Greek (and to show Jacob's prominence in the Christian movement of that time).

Flavius Josephus: Antiquities of the Jews Book 20, Chapter 9:1[7]

And now Caesar, upon hearing the death of Festus, sent Albinus into Judea, as procurator. But the king deprived Joseph of the high priesthood, and bestowed the succession to that dignity on the son of Ananus, who was also himself called Ananus. Now the report goes that this eldest Ananus proved a most fortunate man; for he had five sons who had all performed the office of a high priest to God, and who had himself enjoyed that dignity a long time formerly, which had never happened to any other of our high priests. But this younger Ananus, who, as we have told you already, took the high priesthood, was a bold man in his temper, and very insolent; he was also of the sect of the Sadducees, who are very rigid in judging offenders, above all the rest of the Jews, as we have already observed; when, therefore, Ananus was of this disposition, he thought he had now a proper opportunity. Festus was now dead, and Albinus was but upon the road; so he assembled the sanhedrin of judges, and *brought before them the brother of Jesus, who was called Christ, whose name was James, and some others; and when he had formed an accusation against them as breakers of the law,* he delivered them to be stoned: but as for those who seemed the most equitable of the citizens, and such as were the most uneasy at the breach of the laws, they disliked what was done; they also sent to the king, desiring him to send to Ananus that he should act so no more, for that what he had already done was not to be justified; nay, some of them went also to meet Albinus, as he was upon his journey from Alexandria, and informed him

7. http://data.perseus.org/citations/urn:cts:greekLit:tlg0526.tlg001.perseus-eng1:1. pr.

that it was not lawful for Ananus to assemble a sanhedrin without his consent. Whereupon Albinus complied with what they said, and wrote in anger to Ananus, and threatened that he would bring him to punishment for what he had done; on which king Agrippa took the high priesthood from him, when he had ruled but three months, and made Jesus, the son of Damneus, high priest.

This is useful in being the only (reliable) non-Christian reference to Jesus of Nazareth from a contemporary source. According to traditional Christian and most modern scholarly estimates (in the early 30s CE) Josephus would have been born a few years after the death of Jesus. This text places the death of James, the brother of Jesus in the 60s CE. Interestingly, the text also points to the popularity of the name Jesus at the time, considering we see that the high priesthood was transferred to Jesus, son of Dammeus. The question is, is Jesus the brother of James, *that Jesus*, the very one who inspired Christianity?

Other historical references do not say much about Jesus, but do establish that there was a group of people following him in the mid-first century CE. Tacitus relates a story about a situation in Rome where Nero blamed the Christians, but Tacitus only reveals that the Christians were followers of a "Christus." He does not know of any other name for the founder of the Christian sect, so Tacitus' revelation that there was a certain "Christus" is, ultimately, not very helpful.

> *Tacitus, Annals 15.44*
> Nero fastened the guilt . . . on a class hated for their abominations, called Christians by the populace. Christus, from whom the name had its origin, suffered the extreme penalty during the reign of Tiberius at the hands of . . . Pontius Pilatus, and a most mischievous superstition, thus checked for the moment, again broke out not only in Judaea, the first source of the evil, but even in Rome. . . .

Pliny does more to establish the existence of Christians than Christ, noting the practices of the early Christian communities. This is helpful information for a study on the beliefs and practices of Christians in the second century, but does not tell us much about Jesus, other than that by that time the Christians regard him as a god.

> *Pliny, Letters, transl. by William Melmoth, rev. by W.M.L. Hutchinson (Cambridge: Harvard Univ. Press, 1935), vol. II, X:96, cited in Habermas, The Historical Jesus, 199.*

They were in the habit of meeting on a certain fixed day before it was light, when they sang in alternate verses a hymn to Christ, as to a god, and bound themselves by a solemn oath, not to any wicked deeds, but never to commit any fraud, theft or adultery, never to falsify their word, nor deny a trust when they should be called upon to deliver it up; after which it was their custom to separate, and then reassemble to partake of food – but food of an ordinary and innocent kind.

Lucian confirms some of the data given by Pliny, i.e. that Jesus was worshiped as a god. Lucian is unique in that he regarded Jesus as a lawgiver. Lucian's account adds further to a sociological understanding of the nature of Christian community, but does not tell us anything about Jesus.

> *Lucian, "The Death of Peregrine", 11–13, in The Works of Lucian of Samosata, transl. by H.W. Fowler and F.G. Fowler, 4 vols. (Oxford: Clarendon, 1949), vol. 4., cited in Habermas, The Historical Jesus, 206.*
>
> The Christians . . . worship a man to this day—the distinguished personage who introduced their novel rites, and was crucified on that account. . . . [It] was impressed on them by their original lawgiver that they are all brothers, from the moment that they are converted, and deny the gods of Greece, and worship the crucified sage, and live after his laws.

The historical record is scant and offers little solace to those seeking to find a concrete reference to Jesus. Our best proof is a confirmation of the Greek translation of his name, *Iesous*. However, the early Rabbinic traditions establish that Jesus was known to the Rabbis as Yeshua *ben Pantera*, so our next question must be: who was Pantera?

Who Were Jesus' Parents?

I N Talmudic discourse, topics are brought up through association with other topics in trying to arrive at a legal conclusion. The Talmud is not a historical treatise or even a unified narrative, but rather a series of discussions about the legal topics in the Mishnah. Its primary concern is law but it has quite a bit to say about a variety of other topics. The Talmud provides some details about Jesus' parents, although the references are more polemical than the Tosefta's records.

The issue of Jesus' parentage has been one that has been addressed by many authors, including the Gospel authors themselves. Two of the four canonical Gospels (Mark and John) are not concerned about the issue, likely for different reasons and exhibiting different theologies. However, Matthew and Luke adopt the idea of the virgin birth to address Jesus' parentage, likely in response to Mark who refers to Jesus in this manner, "Is not this the carpenter, *the son of Mary* and brother of James and Joses and Judas and Simon, and are not his sisters here with us?" (Mark 6:3). Jesus is also often referred to as the "son of Mary" in the Qur'an. However, it would have been more common to refer to a person as *son of X*, so in Jesus' case we might expect him to be called *Yeshu(a) ben Yosef, unless Joseph was not his father.* It seems that most traditions (save a few Christian heresies) adopted the idea that Joseph was not Jesus' father. The question then naturally arises, *who was his father?* The Gospels (and the Qur'an) assume that he had no earthly father and was conceived by the Holy Spirit.

One of the Talmudic discussions of Jesus' parentage occurs in a discussion about witnesses in the case of a crime punishable by death in the Torah. The procedure brings up "ben Stada from Lod" who was hanged on

Passover Eve; *ben Setada* is assumed to refer to Jesus the Nazarene for a variety of reasons. The Rabbis then discuss who Jesus' father was. The name *ben Setada* implies that his father was a man named Setada. However, the Rabbis have a tradition of calling him *ben Pandera* (not Joseph). The assumption is that Mary was conceived by another man named Pandeira but that she also had a husband, perhaps named Setada. However, the Rabbis have a tradition that Mary's husband was Pappos ben Yehuda (not Joseph). Therefore, *Setada* might be a reference to his mother. But his mother's name was *Miriam!* Ah, it must be that *Setada* was a nickname! And the explanation is, "This one strayed [*setat da* in Aramaic] from her husband", which was a tradition in Pumbedita (in Babylonia).[1]

> *Sanhedrin 67a*
>
> **As it is taught** in a *baraita*: **And** with regard to **all the rest of those liable to** receive the **death** penalty **by Torah** law, the court **does not hide** witnesses in order **to** ensnare **them** and punish them **except for this** case of an inciter.
>
> **How** does the court **do this to him?** The agents of the court **light a candle for him in an inner room, and** they **place witnesses for him in an outer room** in the dark, **so that they can see him and hear his voice but he cannot see them. And the other** person, whom the inciter had previously tried to incite, **says to him: Say what you said to me** when we were **in seclusion. And he says to him** again that he should worship the idol. **And the other** person **says to him: How can we forsake our God in Heaven and worship idols?** If the inciter **retracts** his suggestion, **that is good. But if he says: This** idol worship **is our duty, and this** is what **suits us, the witnesses, who are listening from outside, bring him to court, and** they **have him stoned.**
>
> **And** the court **did the same to** an inciter named **ben Setada, from** the city of **Lod, and they hanged him on Passover eve.**
>
> The Gemara asks: Why did they call him **ben Setada, when he was the son of Pandeira? Rav Ḥisda says:** Perhaps his mother's **husband,** who acted as his father, was named **Setada,** but his mother's **paramour,** who fathered this *mamzer,* was named **Pandeira.** The Gemara challenges: But his mother's **husband was Pappos ben Yehuda,** not Setada. **Rather,** perhaps **his mother** was named **Setada,** and he was named ben Setada after her. The Gemara challenges: But **his mother was Miriam, who braided women's hair.** The Gemara explains: That is not a contradiction; Setada was

1. This sort of reconciliation of contradictory statements is common in the Talmud, Schäfer, Peter. *Jesus in the Talmud.*

merely a nickname, **as they say in Pumbedita: This one strayed** [setat da] **from her husband.**

The Talmud's details about Jesus are remarkably different from the Gospel accounts, so much so that many have assumed that this is a different Jesus in the Talmud. The differences are astounding, but I will explain why I do not think that necessarily implies that these are different people. First, the geography is different. Jesus is presumed to be from Lod, not Nazareth.[2] However, the connection of Jesus to Nazareth does not seem to happen within Christian texts until the advent of the Gospel of Mark, because Paul never mentions Nazareth (nor does he mention much of anything about Jesus' historical life). Nazareth is not mentioned in other places either by the Rabbis or historians such as Josephus, which implies that either it didn't exist or it was a tiny town.[3] It might have been that *Notzri*, Jesus' title in the Talmud, referred to something else, rather than his birthplace.[4]

Whatever the case, we have two traditions about Jesus, something which is frequent, even in Christian literature. Second, there is quite a bit of confusion about Jesus' father: was he Stada, Pandeira, or Pappos ben Yehuda? The Rabbis seem to agree that Miriam, who braided women's hair (*magdala*), had a husband, Pappos ben Yehuda, and a lover, Pandeira. This is the Rabbis' answer to the question of the lack of reference to Jesus' father. However, the husband, Pappos ben Yehuda, brings us to the third major difference: the chronology. We will see later texts that place Yeshu in the time of Alexander Yannai, who was the Hasmonean King of Israel from 103–76 BCE, whereas Pappos ben Yehuda lived in the second century CE and was a contemporary of Akiva. This is a contradiction, but not uncommon. Even within the Gospels themselves, Jesus was either born in 4 BCE (Matthew) or 6 CE (Luke) and either died around 30 CE or around 36 CE, after the death of John the Baptist in 35 CE. The Ebionites, a first-century Jewish Christian sect, also placed Jesus during the first century BCE, according to Epiphanius' *Panarion*. We could try to resolve the issue by saying there were two Yeshus or two Papposes, but it could be that the association of

---

2. The gospels of Matthew 2:1–9 and Luke 2:1–21 place Jesus' birth in Bethlehem, closer to Lod than to Nazareth, as John says, "Surely the Messiah does not come from Galilee, does he? Has not the scripture said that the Messiah is descended from David and comes from Bethlehem, the village where David lived?" John 7:41–2.

3. Salm, René. *NazarethGate* maintains that Nazareth did not exist in the first century CE.

4. We will return to this issue later.

Pappos ben Yehuda, who locked up his unfaithful wife, was associated with Miriam Magdala.[5]

Ḥagigah 4b

When Rav Yosef reached this verse, he cried: "But there are those swept away without justice" (Proverbs 13:23). **He said: Is there one who goes before his time** and dies for no reason? The Gemara answers: **Yes, like this** incident of **Rav Beivai bar Abaye, who would be frequented** by the company of **the Angel of Death** and would see how people died at the hands of this angel. The Angel of Death **said to his agent: Go** and **bring me,** i.e., kill, **Miriam** the **raiser,** i.e., braider, of **women's hair. He went,** but instead **brought him Miriam, the raiser of babies.**

The Angel of Death **said to him: I told you** to bring **Miriam, the raiser** of **women's hair.** His agent **said to him: If so, return her** to life. **He said to him: Since you** have already **brought her, let her be counted** toward the number of deceased people. Apparently, this woman died unintentionally. Rav Beivai asked the agent: **But** as her time to die had not yet arrived, **how were you able** to kill **her?** The agent responded that he had the opportunity, as **she was holding a shovel in her hand and** with it she **was lighting**

Tosafot, Ḥagigah 4b[6]

The Angel of Death was with him: he related what had already happened, for this about Miriam the dresser of women's hair took place in the time of the second temple, for she was the mother of a certain person.

Jesus' parentage brings up the issue of *mamzerut* (illegitimacy), which is mentioned in the Mishnah Yevamot: that is to say, if Jesus was conceived by Miriam and her lover, he would be considered a *mamzer* ('bastard') under Jewish law. The repercussions of this are serious. Under rabbinic law, he would not be permitted to marry other Israelites, only other *mamzerim.* His lineage would be tainted by that for generations.

Within a discussion of who counts as a *mamzer,* Shimon ben Azzai states, "I found a scroll of genealogical records in Jerusalem, and it was written on it, 'So-and-so is a *mamzer* [having been born] from an adulterous

---

5. Schäfer, P. *Jesus in the Talmud* (pp. 15–17) mentions Eruvin 100b's qualification of a "bad woman" as "[she who] grows long hair like Lilith."

6. The Tosafot is a medieval commentary on the Talmud from France. While it is a late text, it reveals the thinking around this passage among Ashkenazi Jews.

woman.'" Shimon ben Azzai was a third generation tanna, a student of Yehoshua ben Chananiah and a contemporary of Rabbi Akiva.

> *Mishnah, Yevamot 4:13*
>
> **Which** offspring of forbidden relations have the status of **a** mamzer? It is the offspring of a union with **any next of kin that is subject to** a Torah prohibition that **he should not engage in sexual relations** with them; this is **the statement of Rabbi Akiva.** Shimon HaTimni says: It is the offspring of a union with **any** forbidden relation **for which one is liable to** receive karet **at the hand of Heaven. And the** halakha **is in accordance with his statement. Rabbi Yehoshua says:** It is the offspring of a union with **any** forbidden relation **for which one is liable to** receive **court**-imposed **capital punishment. Rabbi Shimon ben Azzai said: I found a scroll** recording people's **lineages in Jerusalem, and it was written in it** that **so-and-so is a** mamzer **from** an adulterous union with **a married woman,** a sin punishable by court-imposed capital punishment. The only reason for the scroll to state the reason that this individual is a *mamzer* is in order **to support the statement of Rabbi Yehoshua.**

It is hard to know if these references relate to Jesus or not. Whether or not they do, it shows a development in how the Rabbis thought about Jesus. From the earlier records, he was remembered in association with healing. As time developed, the Rabbis see him as a mamzer and the product of infidelity. I think it is more likely this is a reaction to Christian doctrine than any specific historical memories on the part of the Rabbis. They interacted with Christians in their lives in Palestine and Babylon and would have been familiar with the general Christian message. This reads as a response to the virgin birth story, rather than an attempt to produce an accurate historical memory.

We now know what Jesus' name was and who his parents (likely) were. We must now look at an important part of Jesus' story in the Talmud: his relationship to his teacher. This relationship will also help us establish what kind of Jew Jesus was.

What Kind of Jew Was Jesus and Who Was His Teacher?

J ESUS THE MAN IS remembered in a specific way in the Jewish tradition, like other members of the rabbinic tradition: he is remembered as the student of a great rabbi, Yehoshua ben Peraḥyah, who was *nasi* of the Sanhedrin. This was the highest-ranking official in the Sanhedrin, recognized even by the Romans as the Patriarch of the Jews. It is perhaps for this reason that Jesus was remembered as being "close to the government" (Sanhedrin 43a). Rabbi Yehoshua with Rabbi Nittai of Arbela were the second of the five *zugot* (pairs) who were instrumental in the transmission of oral tradition in the foundation of rabbinic Judaism. Not much is known about Rabbi Yehoshua ben Peraḥyah, besides his relationship with his famous student, which is also scant in details. Two teachings are preserved in his name, one *aggadic* and one *halakhic*.[1] The teaching found in Pirke Avot[2] (the Chapter of the Fathers) is especially poignant when one analyzes the later incident with Jesus, his student.

> *Pirke Avot 1:4*
> Yehoshua ben Perachiah and Nittai the Arbelite received [the Torah] from them. Yehoshua ben Perachiah says, "Set up a teacher for yourself. And get yourself a companion-disciple. And give everybody the benefit of the doubt.

1. *Aggadic* refers to non-legal material in the Talmud, which can be commentary on biblical text, parables, or other such non-legal material. *Halakhic* refers to legal commentary, with the aim of arriving at a legal decision with regards to an aspect of Jewish law.

2. A section of the Mishnah that is completely aggadic or non-legal and presents Jewish ethics on a number of themes.

Rabbi Yehoshua's teaching in Pirke Avot highlights the importance of the teacher-student relationship. The last line is particularly meaningful after he was accused of *not* giving Yeshu[a] the benefit of the doubt in a particular incident. After that incident, his teaching will forever be remembered as exhorting people to treat others fairly.

Another *aggadic* teaching preserved in his name has to do with the issue of power. In the *baraita*, Yehoshua discusses the position of *nasi*, a powerful position in that time. The discussion in the preceding *sugya* examines a point in the *mishnah* about high priests who serve "for something else," amounting to idolatry, and how this disqualifies them. This leads to a discussion on Onias, one of the High Priests, which devolves into a discourse about power itself. Here we present the full *sugya* which includes Rabbi Yehoshua's statement and a follow-up proof text from the life of Saul in 1 Samuel. Saul initially fled from authority, but once he had it, he tried to kill David. Likewise, Rabbi Yehoshua had a similar experience of becoming Nasi.

> *Menaḥot 109b*
>
> As a corollary to the statement of the Sages with regard to one who is jealous and wants the position of another, **it is taught** in a *baraita* that **Rabbi Yehoshua ben Peraḥya said: Initially,** in response to **anyone who would say** to me: **Ascend to** the position of *Nasi*, **I would tie him up and place him in front of a lion** out of anger for his suggestion. **Now** that I have become the *Nasi*, in response to **anyone who tells me to leave** the position, **I would throw a kettle** [kumkum] **of boiling** water **at him** out of anger at his suggestion.
>
> It is human nature that after one ascends to a prestigious position he does not wish to lose it. **As** evidence of this principle, **Saul** initially **fled from** the kingship, as he did not wish to be king, as stated in the verse: "When they sought him he could not be found ... Behold he has hidden himself among the baggage" (I Samuel 10:21–22).

With regard to his *halakhic* teachings, one unique teaching survives and a disagreement (*maḥloket*) is preserved in the Mishnah where Yehoshua disagrees with Yosef ben Yohanan about whether or not to lay hands on a sacrificial animal on a Festival. This debate preserves the voices of several rabbis from different generations, meaning it was an important disagreement among the earlier Sages.

> Mishnah, *Ḥagigah 2:2*

> **Yosei ben Yo'ezer says not to place** one's hands on offerings before slaughtering them on a Festival because this is considered performing labor with an animal on a Festival. His colleague, **Yosef ben Yoḥanan, says to place** them; **Yehoshua ben Peraḥya says not to place** them; **Nitai HaArbeli says to place** them; **Yehuda ben Tabbai says not to place** them; **Shimon ben Shataḥ says to place** them; **Shemaya says to place** them; **Avtalyon says not to place** them. **Hillel and Menaḥem did not disagree** with regard to this issue. **Menaḥem departed** from his post, and **Shammai entered** in his stead. **Shammai says not to place** them; **Hillel says to place** them. **The first** members of each pair **served as Nasi, and their counterparts** served as **deputy** Nasi.

His only unique *halakhic* teaching relates to another aspect of his life. He fled the Land of Israel to reside in Alexandria, Egypt, with his student, Jesus, during a difficult moment in the Holy Land. The content of the teaching is not necessarily important for the remainder of our work here, but it is important in that it establishes his connection, and therefore, Jesus' connection, to Egypt.

> *Tosefta, Makhshirin 3:4*
> "Joshua b. Peraḥyah said: wheat coming from Alexandria is impure because of their antlia (ἀντλία, watering device). The Sages said: If so, they shall be impure for Joshua b. Peraḥyah and pure for all Israel"

This was Jesus' teacher according to the Talmud. One can see he was well situated within the rabbinic circle, offering both *halakhic* and *aggadic* teaching. Several of his statements can best be understood as reacting to the Jesus episode. In fact, there is one other famous midrashic text in the Talmud where we see an interaction between Jesus and Yehoshua, and I will be discussing that later in the book because it merits a full discussion in its own right.

JOHN THE BAPTIST

John the Baptist is a figure of prominence in Christian sources surrounding the origins of Jesus of Nazareth. In Christian belief he is a prophetic voice that occupies the same role as Elijah in the Jewish traditions around the messiah. The narrative begins in the Gospel of Mark, as John is absent in Paul's letters. This begs the question as to why Paul did not mention John at all. We will only examine John the Baptist in the Gospel of Mark, with some reference to the later developments in the story in later Gospels. The Synoptics largely follow the same tradition, with some modification and with the caveat that Luke has a nativity story for John the Baptist, as well as for Jesus himself.

John appears "in the wilderness" and proclaims a baptism of repentance. John's association with baptism—or immersion (Hebrew, *tebilah*), because it does not refer to the Christian ritual—is strong, both in the Gospels and in Josephus. All of the Gospel stories connect John to Jesus, although in different ways. The earliest account in Mark links Jesus to John by placing Jesus *within* John's movement, as Jesus comes to John to receive baptism (for the remission of sins). Later Gospel authors correct this "problem": how could Jesus, the sinless Savior, need baptism for the repentance of sins? In Mark, John does not really recognize Jesus as "the One" (nor does he strongly do so in any of the Synoptics—John is a different story). It might be that in early Pauline Christian groups, the idea that Jesus was sinless had not yet worked itself out fully, meaning there would be no real problem with Jesus receiving baptism for the forgiveness of sins.

John's message is simple: the Jews need to repent, and to be baptized to symbolize that repentance. He was an apocalyptic prophet who saw the imminent arrival of the Messiah. He also dressed the part, looking like a prophet of old.

> *Mark 1:4–11*
> John the baptizer appeared in the wilderness, proclaiming a baptism of repentance for the forgiveness of sins. And people from the whole Judean countryside and all the people of Jerusalem were going out to him, and were baptized by him in the river Jordan, confessing their sins. Now John was clothed with camel's hair, with a leather belt around his waist, and he ate locusts and wild honey. He proclaimed, "The one who is more powerful than I is coming after me; I am not worthy to stoop down and untie the thong of his sandals. I have baptized you with water; but he will baptize you with the Holy Spirit." In those days Jesus came from Nazareth of Galilee and was baptized by John in the Jordan. And just as he was coming up out of the water, he saw the heavens torn apart and the Spirit descending like a dove on him. And a voice came from heaven, "You are my Son, the Beloved; with you I am well pleased."

Josephus adds to the historical portrait of John, placing him within a historical context during the reign of Herod Antipas, who executed him.

Josephus adds that John preached virtue and morality so that Jews would show righteousness in their lives. He corroborates the association of John with immersion, and notes that the immersion was a purification of the body and the soul. John had a large following among the crowds of that time.

> *Josephus, Antiquities Book 18, 5:2*
> Now some of the Jews thought that the destruction of Herod's [Antipas's] army came from God, and that very justly, as a punishment of what he did against John, that was called the Baptist: for Herod slew him, who was a good man, and *commanded the Jews to exercise virtue, both as to righteousness towards one another, and piety towards God, and so to come to baptism; for that the washing [with water] would be acceptable to him, if they made use of it, not in order to the putting away [or the remission] of some sins [only], but for the purification of the body; supposing still that the soul was thoroughly purified beforehand by righteousness.* Now when [many] others came in crowds about him, for they were very greatly moved [or pleased] by hearing his words, Herod, who feared lest the great influence John had over the people might put it into his power and inclination to raise a rebellion, (for they seemed ready to do any thing he should advise,) thought it best, by putting him to death, to prevent any mischief he might cause, and not bring himself into difficulties, by sparing a man who might make him repent of it when it would be too late. Accordingly he was sent a prisoner, out of Herod's suspicious temper, to Macherus, the castle I before mentioned, and was there put to death. Now the Jews had an opinion that the destruction of this army was sent as a punishment upon Herod, and a mark of God's displeasure to him.

Immersion was a part of some Jewish movements of the time, and was noted in the Qumran community. It is significant that immersion is described as the "waters of repentance." As it must have been an element present in a number of different movements who operated in the same space as did John's movement.

> *Serech HaYachad, or Community Rule (1QS 3:6–9):*
> For it is by the spirit of the true counsel of God that are atoned the paths of man, all his iniquities, so that he can look at the light of life. And it is by the holy spirit of the community, in its truth, that he is cleansed of all his iniquities. And by the spirit of uprightness and of humility his sin is atoned. And by the compliance of his soul with all the laws of God his flesh is cleansed by being

sprinkled with cleansing waters *and being made holy with the waters of repentance.*

Why is John the Baptist not mentioned in the Talmud? The Christian Gospels maintain that John was a relative of Jesus and quite acquainted with him. Modern scholars often presume that Jesus was a disciple of John. Josephus mentions John, but not in connection to Jesus. The Talmud does not know him at all. John's movement is mentioned in the Talmud[3] but not John himself.

If the rabbinic narrative contains traces of memories of the historical Jesus, how did John come to be associated with Jesus?

It seems that the Gospel author of Mark knew that Jesus was associated as the disciple of another teacher (as remembered in the Jewish tradition with Yehoshua ben Peraḥyah). The Gospel author also knew that Galilee was a hotbed of messianic activity in the generation before him, supposing a 70 CE date. He had also likely heard of John the Baptist. It is also quite likely that other early Christian groups were baptists in one way or the other. He must have woven together these ideas and other possible traditions to create the story we now have in his Gospel.

John the Baptist is associated with other traditions beyond Christianity, most notably Islam and the Mandaean religion, which claims him as their main prophet. The Rabbis do not preserve any memories of John the Baptist by name. The Mandaeans are a Gnostic group that still exists today and claims to be descendants from the first-century Nazoraeans and John the Baptist. They believe that the disciples of John the Baptist left Palestine in the first century CE and made their way to Media in modern Iran.

There are some interesting theories around the person of John the Baptist. Robert Price has floated the idea that Jesus is the same as John. Price notes that Jesus associates himself with John throughout the Gospel traditions.[4] Others around Jesus believed he was John raised from the dead (Mark 14:2). He postulates a process of bifurcation where the original group of John the Baptist split between a group dedicated to the martyred John, who awaited the coming of the kingdom (Luke 17:20) and a group who believed that he had risen from the dead. The latter group bestowed upon John the title of "Yeshua" (salvation) because *he* had saved people from their sins and, over time, this title became a name. The former group

---

3. This will be discussed later.

4. Mark 11:28–30; Matthew 11:16–19

became the Mandaeans, who rejected Jesus as a false messiah (in lieving in a spiritual messiah) and the latter became Christians.

The Christian movement, according to Price's theory, worke sions of John into the Gospel of Mark to explain why John the Baptist haa not joined Jesus' movement—because he had died before it truly began. The Gospel cements a strong relationship between the two charismatic leaders, which might have been a way to entice John's disciples to join their movement.

James Tabor postulates that John and Jesus worked together as part of the same apocalyptic, messianic movement, and reads the Gospel accounts of Jesus being baptized by John as indications of Jesus joining the John movement. When John died, Jesus became the leader of this group, which sought the kingship for Jesus. However, upon Jesus' death, the presidency of the group passed to Jesus' brother, Jacob (James). He sees the list of "Christian" bishops in Jerusalem, who were all Jewish until the Bar Kokhba revolt, as being a council of twelve that helped James and his successors lead the movement.[5]

It is accepted by both Christian and Jewish narratives that Jesus had a teacher. The difference in the identity of that teacher reveals how each narrative sees Jesus.

The fact that Jesus had a rabbinic teacher in the Talmudic narrative reveals quite a bit about him as a person, as well as his station in life. If Jesus was a student of the *Nasi* and one of the most well-known rabbis of his age, he could not be a country bumpkin from the middle-of-nowhere town, Nazareth. This is probably a later misreading of the term, *Notsri*, which might better be related to the word for watchers or guardians, and was likely a sectarian designation. It became something of a nickname for Jesus, considering he was not maintained in the community of Rabbis. This explains why the rabbinic tradition never associates him with Nazareth.

The memory of Jesus having a teacher is the origin of the stories of John the Baptist in the Gospels, which are reworked to fit the Gospel writers' chronology. Mark, writing after 70 CE, knew that Jesus came "before" him. He sought to put the birth of Jesus seventy years before the destruction of the Temple.[6] Secondly, Jesus must have been a wealthy man, who studied in the important *yeshivot* of his age, according to the Talmudic narrative. He must have learned the oral traditions of the Rabbis and risen through

5. Tabor, *Jesus Dynasty*.

6. Lawrence, Michael, *Seventy*.

the ranks to be able to be counted as Rabbi Yehoshua's student. The Gospels distance Jesus from this aspect of formal learning at the time. For example, the story of the young Jesus at the Temple, discussing and asking questions about Jewish Law (Luke 2:41–52) is presented as an aberration, resulting from Jesus' youth in that story.[7]

The relationship between the Pharisees and the Rabbis is shrouded in mystery, but it is generally thought that they had some genetic relationship, even if it is not clear what exactly that was. If Jesus was remembered as having a Rabbinic teacher, he would be placed within the Pharisaic camp. Who were the Pharisees? And the Sadducees?

PHARISEES AND SADDUCEES

The Pharisees and Sadducees derived their power from different sources:[8] The Sadducees' power came through the right of inheritance, as the priestly class (although some priests were Pharisees by conviction or necessity, due to their popularity). The Pharisees, on the other hand, derived their power from erudition and skill in legal interpretation.

The Pharisees regarded the Torah as having two components—one written and one oral—and they derived new laws through a logical and rhetorical system from the written and oral Torah. The Pharisees distinguished or separated themselves (*perushim* in Hebrew, "separate") by their distinct practice of the law. They regarded the paying of tithes and ritual impurity as of primary importance and dedicated great energy to keeping those laws. Throughout the Mishnah, we can see the Pharisaic avoidance of the *ame aratzim* (the people of the land, often translated as "ignoramuses"), those who did not follow Pharisaic custom. Pharisees had numerous rules and regulations as to how they interacted with an *am ha aretz*. They formed a type of club, which held high esteem for other members of the club. They called each other *haver* ('friend') and opened membership to anyone, perhaps a reason for their popularity. There was a type of egalitarianism in their organization, in that both the scholar and uneducated Pharisee were treated as friends.

The Sadducees were not as large in number as the Pharisees.[9] They are believed to have descended from Zadok the priest, which the Rabbinic

---

7. This observation was made by my editor, Dr. Amanda Haste.

8. It seems that there were varieties of Pharisees, some very ascetic in nature.

9. According to Josephus, who is our only contemporary source, besides the New

tradition places in the time of Antigonos of Sokho, one of the pairs of *zugot*, although their origin could be earlier, coming out of the priestly aristocracy during the Hasmonean times. This dynasty removed the Zadokite priests from power and this could have forced them into a minority opposition group.[10]

The Sadducees were both politically and later religiously opposed to the Pharisees. For political purposes, the Sadducees represented the aristocracy, whereas the Pharisees represented a lesser class, although still with political and economic power. The Sadducees rejected the Pharisaic "traditions of the elders" (oral Law) but did maintain their own traditions in interpreting the Torah. They had a parallel "Book of Decrees" which explained their interpretation of the Torah.

Still, they regarded only the written law as binding for religious practice. They denied the resurrection of the dead and the immortality of the soul. These beliefs suited the aristocratic membership, who did not suffer in their earthly lives, and had no reason to postpone enjoyment for the afterlife. In contrast, the Pharisees, representing lower classes, held membership of the less fortunate who suffered throughout their earthly lives, in hopes of a resurrection and spiritual paradise. As noted throughout the Talmud, the Pharisees and Sadducees differed on twelve points of ritual and law.

The Pharisees and Sadducees could be seen as resembling political parties in Greco-Roman Israel, both occupying positions of power in that society and influencing the practice of religion by the lower classes. In Josephus they are often mentioned together, as being political and religious rivals.

> *Josephus: Of the War 2 8:14*
> But then as to the two other orders at first mentioned, the Pharisees are those who are esteemed most skilful in the exact explication of their laws, and introduce the first sect. These ascribe all to fate [or providence], and to God, and yet allow, that to act what is right, or the contrary, is principally in the power of men; although fate does co-operate in every action. They say that all souls are incorruptible, but that the souls of good men only are removed into other bodies, but that the souls of bad men are subject to eternal punishment.
> But the Sadducees are those that compose the second order, and take away fate entirely, and suppose that God is not concerned

Testament, on these groups.

10. Bader. *Jewish Heroes*, vol I.

in our doing or not doing what is evil; and they say, that to act what is good, or what is evil, is at men's own choice, and that the one or the other belongs so to every one, that they may act as they please. They also take away the belief of the immortal duration of the soul, and the punishments and rewards in Hades. Moreover, the Pharisees are friendly to one another, and are for the exercise of concord, and regard for the public; but the behavior of the Sadducees one towards another is in some degree wild, and their conversation with those that are of their own party is as barbarous as if they were strangers to them. And this is what I had to say concerning the philosophic sects among the Jews.

Josephus: Antiquities 8.1:3–4

Now for the Pharisees, they live meanly, and despise delicacies in diet; and they follow the contract of reason: and what that prescribes to them as good for them they do: and they think they ought earnestly to strive to observe reason's dictates for practice. They also pay a respect to such as are in years: nor are they so bold as to contradict them in any thing which they have introduced. And when they determine that all things are done by fate, they do not take away the freedom from men of acting as they think fit: since their notion is, that it hath pleased God to make a temperament; whereby what he wills is done; but so that the will of man can act virtuously or viciously. They also believe that souls have an immortal vigour in them: and that under the earth there will be rewards, or punishments; according as they have lived virtuously or viciously in this life: and the latter are to be detained in an everlasting prison; but that the former shall have power to revive and live again. On account of which doctrines they are able greatly to persuade the body of the people: and whatsoever they do about divine worship, prayers, and sacrifices, they perform them according to their direction. Insomuch, that the cities give great attestations to them, on account of their entire virtuous conduct, both in the actions of their lives, and their discourses also.

But the doctrine of the Sadducees is this; that souls die with the bodies. Nor do they regard the observation of anything besides what the law enjoins them. For they think it an instance of virtue to dispute with those teachers of philosophy whom they frequent. But this doctrine is received but by a few: yet by those still of the greatest dignity. But they are able to do almost nothing of themselves. For when they become magistrates; as they are unwillingly and by force sometimes obliged to be; they addict themselves to the notions of the Pharisees: because the multitude would not otherwise bear them.

The Rabbis distanced themselves from the Pharisees, although it seems that they were part of the same group, or emerged from the Pharisees. They admonished the Pharisees:

Mishnah Yadayim 4:6
The Sadducees say: we complain against you, Pharisees, because you say that the Holy Scriptures defile the hands, but the books of Homer do not defile the hands. Rabban Yohanan ben Zakkai said: Have we nothing against the Pharisees but this? Behold they say that the bones of a donkey are clean, yet the bones of Yohanan the high priest are unclean. They said to him: according to the affection for them, so is their impurity, so that nobody should make spoons out of the bones of his father or mother.

However, the later Rabbis themselves wanted to distance themselves from the Pharisees, noting seven different types of false Pharisees; this indicates that there was sectarian in-fighting among different groups of Pharisees (presuming that the Rabbis emerged from this group).

Avot De Rabbi Natan 37:4
There are seven types of [false] Pharisees: the Shechemite Pharisee, the Nakfaite Pharisee, the Miktzoite Pharisee, the Machobaite Pharisee, *the false Pharisees mentioned by their locales are meant to indicate a specific type of false piety. The members of Shechem, for example, agreed to circumcise themselves, but only so their prince could marry Jacob's daughter.* the Pharisee for the sake of a profession, the Pharisee who was obligated by marriage, the Pharisee driven by lust, and the Pharisee driven by fear.

The Rabbis noted the increase of asceticism after the destruction of the Temple.

Bava Batra 60b
The Sages taught in a *baraita* (*Tosefta, Sota* 15:11): **When the Temple was destroyed a second** time, there was **an increase** in the number of **ascetics among** the **Jews,** whose practice was **to not eat meat and to not drink wine. Rabbi Yehoshua joined them** to discuss their practice.

While the Pharisees are missing from the Talmud, the Sadducees are mentioned in several places. They were the rivals of the Pharisees in matters of religion, and likely politics as well. Some of the Rabbis regarded the Sadducees as having the legal status of *gentile*, which also was applied to Samaritans in the Talmud. However, others disagreed because they had close personal interactions with Sadducees.

> *Eruvin 68b*
> The mishna **is incomplete.** It is missing an important element, **and this** is what **it is teaching:** The legal status of **a Sadducee is like** that of **a gentile, and Rabban Gamliel says:** The legal status of **a Sadducee is not like** that of **a gentile. And Rabban Gamliel** further **said:** There was **an incident involving a certain Sadducee who lived with us in** the same **alleyway in Jerusalem,** who renounced his rights in the alleyway before Shabbat, **and Father said to us: Hurry and take out** your **utensils to the alleyway** to establish possession of it **before** he changes his mind and **takes out** his utensils, in which case **he would render it prohibited for you** to use the entire alleyway.
>
> **And** similarly, **wasn't it taught** in a *baraita* that the status of a Sadducee is a matter of dispute between *tanna'im*: If **one lives with a gentile, a Sadducee, or a Boethusian** in the same alleyway, **they render** carrying **prohibited for him. Rabban Gamliel says: A Sadducee or a Boethusian do not prohibit** one from carrying. There was **an incident involving a certain Sadducee who lived with Rabban Gamliel in** the same **alleyway in Jerusalem,** and he renounced his rights to the alleyway before Shabbat. . . .

In a number of cases the Rabbis debated issues of status, as these affect daily life and can affect the status of others. One such case is the issue of *niddah*, ritual impurity brought about by menstruation. The Rabbis enacted several laws to apply the Torah laws around separation during that time. The Sadducees did not accept the Rabbis' legal thinking and authority, relying only on the Written Law, much like the Samaritans. This would affect their legal status for the Rabbis, who would regard them as perpetually impure and unable to engage in normal, sexual relations, until the ritual impurity was removed (and to remove the biblical prohibition of having relations with a woman in the *niddah* state).

> *Niddah 33b*
> **MISHNA:** With regard to **Sadducee girls, when they were accustomed to follow in the ways of their** Sadducee **ancestors their** status **is like** that of **Samaritan women,** whose *halakha* was discussed in the previous mishna. If the Sadducee women **abandoned** the customs of their ancestors in order **to follow in**

the ways of the Jewish people their status **is like** that of **a Jewish woman. Rabbi Yosei says: Their** status **is always like** that of **a Jewish woman, until they will abandon** the ways of the Jewish people in order **to follow in the ways of their** Sadducee **ancestors.**

The Sadducees' denial of the Oral Law caused a number of problems with their Pharisee brethren around various matters of legal interpretation:

Menaḥot 65a
The emissary asks **three times with regard to each and every matter, and** the assembly **says to him: Yes, yes, yes.** The mishna asks: **Why do I** need those involved to publicize each stage of the rite **to that extent?** The mishna answers: It is **due to the Boethusians, as they** deny the validity of the Oral Law and **would say: There is no harvest of the** omer **at the conclusion of the** first **Festival** day of Passover unless it occurs at the conclusion of Shabbat. . . .

Rosh Hashanah 22b
Initially, they would accept testimony to determine the start of the **month from any person, and** this continued until the Boethusians began to corrupt the process. **The Sages taught** a *baraita* that describes the decisive incident: **What** was the manner of **the corruption** in which **the Boethusians engaged? Once, the Boethusians tried to mislead the Sages** with regard to the day of the new moon. **They hired two people for four hundred dinars** to testify falsely that they had seen the new moon on the thirtieth day of the month. . . .

Torah scrolls written by Sadducees were not fit for ritual use.

Soferim 1:13
A scroll of the Torah that was written by a Sadducee, an informer, a proselyte, a slave, a woman, a madman or a minor may not be used for the lection. This is the rule: Whosoever cannot act in religious matters on behalf of the public is not permitted to write a scroll of the Torah.

The memories of Jesus in the Talmud place him within the Pharisaic camp, meaning the "mainstream." While the Pharisees and Sadducees were the largest Jewish sects of the time, I would like to mention some other sects that existed around this time, as Jesus' later trajectory brings him perhaps closer to other groups besides the Pharisees.

THE ESSENES AND OTHER MINOR SECTS

The Essenes were less numerous than the Pharisees and Sadducees but have attracted a great deal of attention from scholars due to their proximity to some Christian sects. Josephus mentions this group in *Antiquities* and in further detail in *The Wars of the Jews* (*War*).

> *Josephus: Antiquities 18 1:5*
>
> The doctrine of the Essenes is this; that all things are best ascribed to God. They teach the immortality of souls: and esteem that the rewards of righteousness are to be earnestly striven for. And when they send what they have dedicated to God into the temple, they do not offer sacrifices: because they have more pure lustrations of their own. On which account they are excluded from the common court of the temple: but offer their sacrifices themselves. Yet is their course of life better than that of other men; and they entirely addict themselves to husbandry. It also deserves our admiration, how much they exceed all other men that addict themselves to virtue, and this in righteousness: and indeed to such a degree, that as it hath never appeared among any other men, neither Greeks nor Barbarians, no not for a little time: so hath it endured a long while among them. This is demonstrated by that institution of theirs, which will not suffer any thing to hinder them from having all things in common: so that a rich man enjoys no more of his own wealth, than he who hath nothing at all. There are about four thousand men that live in this way: and neither marry wives, nor are desirous to keep servants: as thinking the latter tempts men to be unjust; and the former gives the handle to domestic quarrels. But as they live by themselves, they minister one to another. They also appoint certain stewards to receive the incomes of their revenues, and of the fruits of the ground; such as are good men, and priests: who are to get their corn, and their food ready for them. They none of them differ from others of the Essenes in their way of living: but do the most resemble those Dacæ, who are called *Polistæ*. [Dwellers in cities.]

The Essenes began in Hasmonean times from the school of Ḥasidim (obviously distinct from later movements of the same name). They regarded martyrdom as a noble cause, and retreated from urban life. They became disengaged after the ascent of the Hasmoneans and regarded them as not sufficiently Jewish in behavior.

The Essenes believed that their own customs would result in a man being filled with the holy spirit, and kept a library of additional books that described their practice and outlook. Some were known as healers and the whole community eschewed sacrifices in favor of daily prayers. They were highly ascetic, rejecting meat and wine and other worldly pleasures and valuing suffering as a spiritual practice. They had high ethical standards for their members as well. Their community was strictly communitarian, rejecting private possessions and holding all in common. They wore the same clothing as well. They held strict *halakhic* standards around the Sabbath, not eating any hot food, like the Rabbis and presumably the Pharisees. They might be related to other immersing sects, due to their practice of daily ritual immersions in the morning.

Several other sects were active during this time, which might have some bearing on the religious context in which Jesus and his movement lived. The Bana'im were a group adjacent to the Essenes in the first century CE, and the name is found in the Mishnah:

> *Mikva'ot 9:6*
> "Garments belonging to the Bana'im may not have a mud stain even upon one side, because these people are very particular concerning the cleanliness of their clothing, and any such spot would prevent the purifying water from actually penetrating the garment as it is usually worn; but with a bor [an unlearned and uncultured man], it matters not if his clothing contain a red spot at the time of dipping, for such a one is not particular about cleanliness."

It is an esoteric passage and other scholars link the group to the so-called Hemerobaptists from the Greek word for "bath" and suggest that this group might have engaged in frequent ritual immersion. The Hemerobaptists, or *Tovele Shaharit* in Hebrew, refers to an immersing group that engaged in daily immersion in the morning. This group likely derived from the Essenes as well and placed particular emphasis on the ritual cleansing before prayer. They are mentioned in the Talmud:

> *Berakhot 22a*
> **Rabbi Yehoshua ben Levi said: What is the essence of those who immerse themselves in the morning?** The Gemara retorts: How can one ask **what is their essence? Isn't he** the one **who said** that **one who experiences a seminal emission is prohibited from** engaging in **matters of Torah** and is required to immerse himself in the morning? Rather, **this is** what **he** meant to **say: What is the essence of** immersion in a ritual bath of **forty** se'a of water when **it is possible** to purify oneself **with nine** kav? Furthermore, **what**

47

is the essence of immersion when **it is** also **possible** to purify oneself by **pouring** water?

Scholars suggest that John the Baptist was likely a member of this group[11], which makes sense given the limited information we know about him. John's movement likely split into different factions after his death (as did that of Jesus). It seems that some of John's disciples are remembered as becoming Christians, which is not unlikely. Also, some formed the group later known as Mandeans. The Jewish Encyclopedia refers to the references to this group in Christian literature,

> *Jewish Encyclopedia*
> "Several early Christian authors make mention of the Hemerobaptists. Hegesippus refers to them as one of the Jewish sects or divisions opposed to Christians; Justin calls them "Baptizers." According to the Christian editor of the *Didascalia* (Apostolic Constitutions 6:6), the Hemerobaptists do not make use of their beds, tables, and dishes until they have cleansed them. This is a misunderstanding of the true purpose of this sect, i.e., bodily cleansing. Another author, Epiphanius, asserts that the Hemerobaptists deny future salvation to persons who do not undergo daily baptism."

Two other minor sects merit mention in our discussion. First, the Hypsistarians were a sect that lived on the Bosphorus in the first century CE. They seem to be a Judaizing sect that observed the Sabbath and dietary laws but deviated from other Jews in that they venerated fire and light and the earth, although there is no record of worshiping these entities. They might be related to other minor sects and the *Yire Shamayim* ("venerators of heaven") as mentioned in other sources. They seem to occupy a place between Christianity and Judaism, even more so than the Ebionites.

The Maghariya were a sect that arose in the first century BCE. It is an Arabic name referring to the "people of the caves", those who kept their sacred writings in the hills of Israel. They seem to have believed that God was above physical matter and might have believed that an intermediary was responsible for the creation. They interpreted anthropomorphic references to God in Torah as actually being references to an angel. There are two surviving works that are attributed to them: the Alexandrian and *Sefer Yadu'a*.

We will see that, according to the Talmudic record, Jesus was not always a Pharisee; he strayed from Pharisaic orthodoxy and ended up leaving the fold. His destiny after that is unclear in the tradition. He was charged

---

11. Also referenced in the early Church Fathers, *Clementine Homilies 2:23*

with practicing sorcery (magic) and inciting others to idolatry. We will see what that *might* mean in later chapters, but it is important to understand the context within Judaism and the various movements that existed. One other group must be mentioned, first, as Jesus is called a messianic figure. However, Jesus is never called that in the Talmud or any Rabbinic literature (in later Jewish literature, he is called a false messiah). To claim to be a messiah could mean that Jesus was a rebel of some kind, seeking to initiate the apocalyptic messianic age and the transformation of the known world. Conversely, it could mean that he sought political rebellion against Rome to start a Jewish kingdom, as the Maccabees had done earlier. For various reasons, we will see that Jesus' movement did not fall into these categories.

Josephus mentions a "fourth philosophy," which scholars sometimes call Zealots. Josephus describes them as agreeing with the Pharisees in most matters, except in the Pharisees' attitude towards Rome, which was mostly conciliatory. This group began with Judas the Galilean, who we will explore below. It seems this group overlapped with the Messianic movement, which included a number of messianic claimants throughout the first century CE.

> *Josephus: Antiquities 18 1:6*
> But of the fourth sect of Jewish philosophy, Judas the Galilean was the author. These men agree in all other things with the Pharisaic notions; but they have an inviolable attachment to liberty; and say that God is to be their only ruler and lord. They also do not value dying any kinds of death; nor indeed do they heed the deaths of their relations and friends: nor can any such fear make them call any man lord. And since this immoveable resolution of theirs is well known to a great many, I shall speak no farther about that matter. Nor am I afraid that any thing I have said of them should be disbelieved: but rather fear that what I have said is beneath the resolution they shew when they undergo pain. And it was in Gessius Florus's time that the nation began to grow mad with this distemper; who was our procurator; and who occasioned the Jews to go wild with it, by the abuse of his authority; and to make them revolt from the Romans. And these are the sects of Jewish philosophy.

THE MESSIAHS[12]

There were several other Jewish messianic movements from around 4 BCE to 100 CE with which to compare Jesus' supposedly messianic movement; the movements mentioned in Josephus' accounts of the history of the period include the movements of Judas son of Ezekias, Simon a slave of King Herod, Anthronges, Menahem, John of Gischala, and Simon bar Giona.

The idea of the Messiah is not entirely biblical, but results from Pharisaic and rabbinic thinking. The bulk of messianic material is developed later in the Tanakh, in the book of Daniel. Here Daniel is giving a prophecy and mentions an "anointed leader" which Rashi[13] links to Cyrus of Persia, but which could also refer to a future messiah.

> Daniel 9:25–26[14]
> You must know and understand: From the issuance of the word to restore and rebuild Jerusalem until the [time of the] anointed leader is seven weeks; and for sixty-two weeks it will be rebuilt, square and moat, but in a time of distress. And after those sixty-two weeks, the anointed one will disappear and vanish. The army of a leader who is to come will destroy the city and the sanctuary, but its end will come through a flood. Desolation is decreed until the end of war.

The word *messiah* (Hebrew, anointed) is applied to the king and high priest in the Hebrew Bible. In Daniel, the anointed one is described as a ruler or prince. This was the core of the later development of the theories about King Messiah, still relevant to both Judaism and Christianity to this day. Several texts in the intertestamental period mention the idea of the messiah, and the idea that he will be of the Davidic line is developed in the Psalm of Solomon (17:21). This text dates from the reign of Herod the Great (37–4 BCE), making it a fairly late text in which the idea is further fleshed out in this important text, whose key ideas I will now highlight.

12. For further exploration of this topic, see: Lenowitz, Harris. *Jewish Messiahs: From the Galilee to Crown Heights*. Oxford University Press, 2001, and Giles, Glenn. "1st Century Messianic Movements." Grabbe, Lester. *An Introduction to Second Temple Judaism: History and Religion of the Jews in the Time of Nehemiah, the Maccabees, Hillel and Jesus*. New York: T & T Clark (2010).

13. Rabbi Shelomo Yitzhaki, a famous 12th century French rabbi, most known for his commentaries on the Hebrew Bible and Talmud. He is known by the acronym, Rashi, Ra[bbi]Sh[elomo]I[tzhaki], a common nomenclature in Jewish sources for famous rabbis.

14. Composed in the second century BCE

Psalm of Solomon 17:26–32[15]

And he will bring together a holy people whom he will lead in righteousness. And he will judge the tribes of the people that have been made holy by the Lord their God. He will not permit unrighteousness to pause among them any longer, and any man who knows wickedness will not live with them. For he will know them that they are all children of their God. He will distribute them in their tribes upon the land; the sojourner and the foreigner will no longer dwell beside them. He will judge peoples and nations in the wisdom of his righteousness. Pause. And he will have gentile nations serving him under his yoke and he will glorify the Lord in [a place] visible [from] the whole earth. And he will cleanse Jerusalem to [reach] a sanctification as [she has] from the beginning so that nations will come from the ends of the earth to see his glory, bringing as gifts her children who had become quite weak, and to see the glory of the Lord with which God has glorified her. And he will be a righteous king over them, taught by God. There will be no unrighteousness among them in his days, for all [will be] holy, and their king [will be] the Lord Messiah.

Here we see several key ideas: the Messiah will be a righteous king who will lead the people in righteousness and banish wickedness from the land. He will judge the tribes of Israel and distribute the land according to tribes, removing the foreigners from the land. The gentile nations will serve under him and he will cleanse Jerusalem. This righteous king will reign in Jerusalem, "purging it from gentiles" (Psalm of Solomon 17:22). He will rule by faith in God and righteousness, who will restore some aspects of the Davidic monarchy and restore Jewish supremacy in the land.

The Qumran community began to develop many ideas about who the messiah was to be. It seems the community was active in the first centuries before the Common Era and disbanded around the time of the first war with the Romans, although those dates are not necessarily agreed upon by all scholars. The Damascus Document mentions the idea of the messiah in many places, most notably noting that the messiah will forgive sins.

Covenant of Damascus 12:23–13:1[16]

Here, however, is the rule for such camp-communities as may come into existence throughout the Era of Wickedness-that is, until the priestly and the lay 'messiah' again assume office.[59] The

15. Composed in the second century BCE

16. The Dead Sea Scrolls were composed sometime between the third century BCE and the first century CE.

people who follow these rules must consist in any given instance of a minimum of ten,[60] and beyond that must be grouped by thousands, hundreds, fifties and tens.

Covenant of Damascus 14:19
And these, in specific form, are the regulations which they are to follow throughout the Era of Wickedness, until the priestly and lay 'messiahs' enter upon their office and expiate their iniquities.

These communities regarded the messiah as a future figure, possibly involving two figures, one priestly and the other royal. However, other traditions at Qumran point to a warrior figure:

1Q Sb 20–27 [The Rule of the Blessing]
[17]The Master shall bless the Prince of the Congregation. . . . May the Lord raise you up to everlasting heights, and as a fortified tower upon a wall! (May you smite the peoples) with the might of your hand and ravage the earth with your scepter; may you bring death to the ungodly with the breath of your lips! (May He shed upon you the spirit of counsel) and everlasting might, the spirit of knowledge and of the fear of God; may righteousness be the girdle (of your loins) and may your reins be girdled (with faithfulness)! May He make your horns of iron and your hooves of bronze; may you toss like a young bull (and trample the peoples) like the mire of the streets! For God has established you as a scepter.

The Messiah is connected to the House of David (4QF1 1:10–11) who will interpret the Law and save Israel.

4QF1 1:10–11 [Psalms]
It states, He is the Branch of David who shall arise with the Interpreter of the Law (to rule) in Zion (at the end) of time. As it is written, I will raise up the tent of David that is fallen (Amos 9:11). That is to say, the fallen tent of David is he who shall arise to save Israel.

Other scrolls support this idea of a Davidic messiah, as in these two examples:

4QPB on Genesis 49:10
The scepter (shall not) depart from the tribe of Judah . . . Whenever Israel rules, there shall (not) fail to be a descendant of David upon the throne. For the ruler's staff is the Covenant of

17. The Dead Sea Scrolls are named by location, 1Q, 4Q, etc. and then by content.

kingship, (and the clans) of Israel are the divisions, until the Messiah of Righteousness comes, the Branch of David. For to him and his seed is granted the Covenant of kingship over his people for everlasting generations which he is to keep . . . the Law with the men of the Community

4QPI on Is. 9:1–3
(Interpreted, this concerns the Branch) of David who shall arise at the end (of days) . . . God will uphold him with (the spirit of might, and will give him) a throne of glory and crown of (holiness) and many-coloured garments . . . (He will put a scepter) in his hand and he shall rule over all the (nations). And Magog . . . and his sword shall judge (all) the peoples.

1 Enoch depicts a future deliverer, "the "Anointed One" (48:10; 52:4), the "Elect One" (49:2, 4; 51:3, 5; 53:6), and the "Righteous One" (53:6)" but does not mention Davidic descent. The text also states, "And he said to me, 'All these things which you have seen shall serve the dominion of his Anointed One, that he may be powerful and mighty on the earth" (1 Enoch 52:4). Additionally:

1 Enoch 48:8–10[18]
At that time downcast in countenance shall the kings of the earth become, and the strong who occupy the land, on account of the deeds of their hands; for on the day of their anguish and affliction they shall not save themselves. And I will give them over into the hands of my elect ones: As stubble in the fire so shall they burn before the face of the holy, as lead in the water shall they sink before the face of the righteous, and no trace of them shall any more be found. And on the day of their affliction there shall be rest on the earth, and before them they shall fall and not rise again: And there shall be no one to take them by his hands and raise them up: For they denied the Lord of Spirits and his Anointed One.

The Testaments of the Twelve Patriarchs[19] presents the doctrine of two messiahs, one from the tribe of Levi (Testament of Reuben 6:7–12) and one from Davidic lineage (Testament of Judah 7:5–6).

Giles summarizes the main points of who the messiah was, according to these various sources: "(1) a king of some sort, (2) a militant ruler, (3) he will restore control of Israel to the Jews, (4) he may have some priestly role,

18. This text was composed in stages from the third to first centuries BCE.
19. The text reached its final form in the second century CE.

(5) he will restore righteousness to the land, and (6) he will probably be a descendant of David or possibly Levi."[20] Messiahs have been noted by failure, which leads to their characteristics of abandonment and ambivalence. The messiah abandons their physical being, diminishing their human nature over a cosmic sense of being, sometimes regarding him as consisting of two or three persons, physical and spiritual. Especially for king-messiahs (as opposed to priest-messiahs), the messiah's parentage and birth are effaced, by not revealing anything of their personal background. Messiahs often assume a new name and neglect their own family, frequently eschewing marriage and typical family life. The messiah's family is his following, as is their home. The messiah's home often rejects him. Interestingly, all Roman-era messiahs are known as Galileans, even if they did not come from there. Many messiahs were lifelong itinerants. They often become lawgivers, either learning and becoming a master of traditional law and building on it or through prophetic revelation. The messiah was a troubled individual, due to his rejection of his own family, leading to potential psychic damage, especially as his mission began to fail.[21]

The messianic movements that existed during the time in which Christians placed Jesus began after the reign of Herod the Great, which ended in 4 BCE. He was a brutal king who brought havoc on his own people, and there were countless messianic claimants and movements at that time. We have records for a few of them, which can help illuminate who these men were and what their goals might have been.

> *Josephus: Antiquities 17 10.8*
> And so Judea was filled with brigandage. Any one might make himself king (*basileus*) as the head of a band of rebels who fell in with, and then would press on to the destruction of the community, causing trouble to few Romans and then only to a smaller degree but bringing the greatest slaughter upon their own people.

Brigands were lower class, who revolted against Rome's taxation and cementing of the priestly aristocracy. The idea of deliverance must have been appealing to them, so much so that they would be willing to fight and die for the cause of freedom from Rome and their collaborators in Jerusalem.

Seeing Jesus' social stature, as presented in the Talmud gives us all the clues we need to dismiss him from the hall of fame of messianic claimants.

20. Giles, "Messianic Movements," p. 10.
21. Lennowitz p. 264ff

Jesus, being "close to the government" and a student of the Nasi, did not come from the peasant class. He was from a wealthy family. Even if what Celsus wrote is true, that his family fell on hard times, they would have been of considerable status. Jesus would not have lowered himself to fight in a peasants' war against Rome; he likely shared the Pharisaic idea of accommodation to Rome to ensure Jewish survival.

Perhaps the first such messianic claimant was Judas the Galilean, who "incited his countrymen to revolt up braiding them as cowards for consenting to pay tribute to the Romans and tolerating mortal masters, after having God for their Lord. This man was a sophist who founded a sect of his own . . . " (War 2:118). This occurred in the year 6 CE and began what is now called the Zealot school within first-century Judaism. Judas believed that only God was the Lord over the Jews and that the Romans could not claim to have any power over God's chosen people.

Josephus comments on the situation of the people after this particular king, and the first messianic movement under Judas son of Ezekias. It seems a natural response to a tyrannical king to seek liberation. This is the context of first-century messianic movements and the crescendo against Rome in 70 CE and later during the Bar Kokhba revolt.

> *Josephus: Antiquities 17 10.5*
> Then there was Judas, the son of the brigand chief Ezekias, who had been a man of great power . . . This Judas got together a large number of desperate men at Sepphoris in Galilee and there made an assault on the royal palace, and having seized all the arms that were stored there, he armed every single one of his men and made off with all the property that had been seized there. He became an object of terror to all men by plundering those he came across in his desire for great possessions and his ambition for royal rank a prize that he expected to obtain not through the practice of virtue but through excessive ill treatment of others.

Judas' revolt began near what became Nazareth, in Sepphoris, one of the larger cities in Galilee. He gathered a group of men to attack a palace and seized its arms; he wanted royal power for himself and seems to have caused as much terror as Herod the Great had done before him. Judas was not afraid to use force or engage in military tactics to bring about his goal, and his movement was by definition militant. However, because Judas wanted to return "property that had been seized there", perhaps there was some sense of justice to his mission. In any case, his actions sparked the messianic fervor at the beginning of the first century CE, and many other movements followed in his footsteps to engage in guerrilla warfare against the Romans in Palestine.

The next messianic figure was Simon, a slave of King Herod, who crowned himself king, by placing the crown on his head. A group of men followed him and proclaimed him king, although this group burned a royal palace in Jericho, which places Simon's activity in Judea rather than Galilee. He engaged in a similar campaign to that of Judas, but his motives seem less attributable to justice and he burned several royal palaces and residences throughout the country.

> *Josephus: Antiquities 17 10.6*
> There was also Simon, a slave of King Herod, but a handsome man, who took pre-eminence by size and bodily strength, and was expected to go farther. Elated by the unsettled conditions of affairs, he was bold enough to place the diadem on his head, and having got together a body of men, he was himself also proclaimed king by them in their madness . . . After burning the royal palace in Jericho, he plundered and carried off the things that had been seized there. He also set fire to many other royal residences in many parts of the country and utterly destroyed them after permitting his fellow rebels to take as booty whatever had been left by them.

Athronges led the third messianic movement as a shepherd. He sought the kingship for himself and eventually crowned himself king and convened a council to draft an action plan. Josephus indicates that he kept power for some time and also engaged in warfare against the Romans and the Jewish king in Palestine, though it is not clear from Josephus' account where Anthronges was based.

> *Josephus: Antiquities 17 10.7*
> This man had the temerity to aspire to the kingship, thinking that if he obtained it, he would enjoy freedom to act more outrageously . . . Athronges himself put on the diadem and held a council to discuss what things were to be done, but everything depended upon his own decision. This man kept his power for a long while, for he had the title of king and nothing to prevent him from doing what he wished. He and his brothers also applied themselves vigorously to slaughtering the Romans and the King's men.

The latter messianic movements sprang up during the revolt against Rome and involved a few different groups, including Menahem, John of

Gischala and Simon son of Giora, who also revolted against the Romans with the Zealots, Sicarii, and the Idumeans.[22]

Menahem was the leader of the Sicarii and related to Judas of Galilee, who began rebelling in 6 CE, and was the founder of the "fourth philosophy"; Menahem and his followers marched to Masada and stole weapons from Herod's arsenal during the War (66–70 CE). Menahem led his men towards Jerusalem and caused the Romans to retreat for a short while (but shortly thereafter Menahem was killed by Eleazer and the Temple guard.[23] The Sicarii retreated to Masada and did not engage in combat until 74 CE when the Romans captured Masada.

The Rabbis knew of a Menahem who was later associated with the same man. He disagreed with the Sages and "left his place" and was replaced by Shammai; the Rabbis did not give a reason, only that he "went astray" (Ḥagigah 16a). This was Abaye's position, however, and Rava added further details: "He departed for the king's service. This is also taught: Menahem departed for the king's service, and eighty pairs of students dressed in silk robes left with him" (16b), meaning he received a royal appointment and did not want to study Torah any further. It is hard to know whether these stories are about the same man, but the Rabbis' reluctance to go into detail does give some credence to the idea. Additionally, Josephus tells us that the Zealots and the Rabbis (or Pharisees) did not disagree on core issues, only in method.

Around the same time John of Gischala was also a prominent messianic figure from the ranks of the Zealots. He was a revolutionary who tried to take over Josephus' command in Galilee[24] and went to Jerusalem during the war to help with the resistance against the Romans.

> *War 4:390*
> aspiring to despotic power, began to disdain the position of mere equality in honors with his peers, and, gradually gathered around him a group of more depraved, broke away from the coalition. Invariably disregarding the decisions of the rest, and issuing imperious orders of his own, he was evidently laying claim to absolute sovereignty"

22. *War* 7:262–270

23. *War* 2:427–428

24. *War* 4:85

Due to his authoritarian nature he did not win all of the Zealots' support. The Romans eventually captured him and took him to Rome, where he served a life sentence.[25]

Simon bar Giora can also be described as a Zealot. He joined the movement at Masada and participated in several raids in that area.

> *War 4:508–513*
> He, on the contrary, was aspiring to despotic power and cherishing high ambitions; accordingly on hearing of the death of Ananus, he withdrew into the hills, where, by proclaiming liberty for slaves and rewards for the free, he gathered around him the villains from every quarter. Having now a strong force, he first overran the villages in the hills, and then through continual additions to his numbers was emboldened to descend into the low lands. And now when he was becoming a terror to the towns, many men of standing were seduced by his strength and career of unbroken success into joining him; and his was no longer an army of mere serfs or brigands, but one including numerous citizen recruits, subservient to his command as to a king . . . His object was evident: he was training his force and making all these preparations for an attack on Jerusalem.

He was successful for a time, as were most of the messiahs, capturing Idumea and marching into Jerusalem; however, the Romans eventually captured him as well.

There are other records of other likely messianic claimants, such as Tholomaeus who "inflicted very severe mischief upon the Idumeans"[26] between 44–46 CE and was executed for his activities. However, it is not clear that he claimed to be a messiah or had any political motives for his campaigns. The following other potential candidates did not claim to be the messiah either (or at least no record survives of such claims). Theudas, mentioned in Acts 5:36, led an army of five hundred men, who were captured and killed.[27] James and Simon, sons of Judas the Galilean were crucified by the Romans around 46–48 CE for "the people to revolt against the Romans while Quirinius was taking the census in Judea."[28] Eleazer ben Dinai and a man called Alexander took revenge on the Samaritans, who had killed a number of Jews; they burned Samaritan villages and killed the

25. *War* 6:434
26. *Antiquities* 20:5
27. *Antiquities* 20:97–99
28. *Antiquities* 20:102

residents, and the Romans mobilized to stop their campaign, which was seen as a rebellion against Rome.[29]

An unnamed Egyptian is also counted as a messianic claimant. He led a group of 30,000 men to the Mount of Olives to take over Jerusalem, but the Romans put down his uprising. There are some who claim that the Egyptian was none other than Jesus. It is important to note that the Egyptian was called a "magician" by Josephus, and some have tried to link Jesus of Nazareth to this mysterious character. It seems he was a prophetic teacher of some kind, who organized a form of opposition to the Romans, which ultimately failed.

> *War 2 13:5*
> But there was an Egyptian false prophet that did the Jews more mischief than the former; for he was a cheat, and pretended to be a prophet also, and got together thirty thousand men that were deluded by him: these he led round about from the wilderness to the mount which was called *the Mount of Olives*, and was ready to break into Jerusalem by force from that place; and if he could but once conquer the Roman garrison, and the people, he intended to domineer over them by the assistance of those guards of his that were to break into the city with him. But Felix prevented his attempt, and met him with his Roman soldiers, while all the people assisted him in his attack upon them, insomuch that when it came to a battle, the Egyptian ran away, with a few others, while the greatest part of those that were with him were either destroyed or taken alive; but the rest of the multitude were dispersed every one to their own homes, and there concealed themselves.

Eliazar, son of Simon, was the last messiah of the first century CE. He became leader of the Zealots during the war with Rome (66–70 CE) and was given command over their group in Jerusalem.[30] Giles notes that he did not claim to be a messiah and the Zealots were more of a democratically inclined group which would have eschewed kingship. He might have tried to fulfill a priestly messianic role, but this is not clear from the historical record.

All of this goes to show the type of movements that were led by the first-century messiahs. None of them fits the picture of Jesus found in the Talmud, or in the Gospels for that matter. In the Talmud, Jesus is assumed to have been a healer and teacher of some kind. However, there are no

29. *War* 2:235
30. *War* 2:565

references to any claim for him to be a messiah, unlike other figures, such as Bar Kokhba, the famous second-century CE messianic figure. To put it simply, *the Rabbis do not remember Jesus as a false messiah, but as a false teacher.*

That leaves two groups to consider. These groups, which overlapped in Antiquity, are magicians and Gnostics. It is my contention that Jesus was a part of both these groups.

THE MAGICIANS AND GNOSTICS

What we term *magic* was probably closer to what ancient people thought of as *religion*, meaning there was not much of a separation between magical practice and devotion to God or the gods, even among Jews and Christians. Therefore, to claim that Jesus was a magician is not a controversial claim nor meant to offend anyone, but rather to proclaim a truth about ancient religion that is uncomfortable to most modern religious people.

First, we must note that archeology points to this fact, as recent findings have shown that magic incantation bowls have been found that read "Christ the magician" from the late second century BCE to the first century CE (an interesting point about dating). These magic incantation bowls seemed to be very common in magical practice during the time.

Although throughout the text, I use the word "magician" to describe Jesus, the word is overladen with modern connotations that distract from its intended meaning. A neutral term *ritual freelance experts* helps alleviate the negative connotations with "magician" that are not intended in this text. These were self-authorized experts in a variety of subjects, including religion. They "practiced asceticism, who were itinerant, who divined, and who boasted ritual expertise . . . the central feature of my category is, again, that the actors it encompasses operated independently of existing institutions to offer skills, teachings, and other practices that involved the direct participation of divine beings."[31] Freelance experts were often associated with cultic voluntary associations and observed to "to form networks with one another, or to develop mutually beneficial relationships with existing religious groups and institutions."[32] The type of religious activity performed by these freelancers involved elements of what is now known as magic, astrology, mystery cults, philosophy, Judaism, and Christianity, and included

31. Wendt, *At The Temple Gate*, p. 12
32. Wendt, *At The Temple Gate*, p. 16

a variety of common ritual acts such as, "prayer and other speech acts, sacrifice and other offerings, divination, purifications, special communal meals, caring for the spirits of ancestors, being initiated (or initiating someone else) into a god's mysteries."[33]

Magic is a serious offense in Jewish law, being condemned in the Torah, making it a *biblical* prohibition, the most serious kind of offense.

> *Deuteronomy 18:10–11*
> No one shall be found among you who makes a son or daughter pass through fire, or who practices divination, or is a soothsayer, or an augur, or a sorcerer, **11** or one who casts spells, or who consults ghosts or spirits, or who seeks oracles from the dead.

However, the Rabbis themselves have a problematic relationship with magical practices. Consider the record of Rabbi Akiva, a student of Rabbi Eliezer, who notes that his teacher taught three hundred laws about witches[34], meaning he had some interest in the subject. However, not many of these laws were preserved, showing the Rabbis' discomfort with the association. The issue of *halakhot* related to cucumbers is a reference to sorcery.

> *Sanhedrin 68a*
> **When Rabbi Eliezer took ill, Rabbi Akiva and his colleagues came to visit him. He was sitting on his canopied bed** [bekinof], **and they were sitting in his parlor** [biteraklin]; they did not know if he would be able to receive them, due to his illness. **And that day was Shabbat eve, and** Rabbi Eliezer's **son Hyrcanus entered to remove his phylacteries,** as phylacteries are not worn on Shabbat. His father **berated him, and he left reprimanded.** Hyrcanus **said to his** father's **colleagues: It appears to me that father went insane,** since he berated me for no reason. Rabbi Eliezer heard this and **said to them: He, Hyrcanus, and his mother went insane. How can they neglect** Shabbat preparations with regard to **prohibitions** punishable by **stoning,** such as lighting the candles and preparing hot food, **and engage in** preparations concerning **prohibitions by rabbinic decree,** such as wearing phylacteries on Shabbat?
> **Since the Sages perceived** from this retort **that his mind was stable, they entered and sat before him at a distance of four cubits,** as he was ostracized (see *Bava Metzia* 59b). It is forbidden to sit within four cubits of an ostracized person.

---

33. Wendt, *At The Temple Gate*, p. 30
34. See also: Tosefta Sanhedrin 11:2; Jerusalem Talmud 7:13

Rabbi Eliezer **said to them: Why have you come? They said to him: We have come to study Torah,** as they did not want to say that they came to visit him due to his illness. Rabbi Eliezer **said to them: And why have you not come until now? They said to him: We did not have spare time.** Rabbi Eliezer **said to them: I would be surprised if these** Sages **die their own death,** i.e., a natural death. Rather, they will be tortured to death by the Romans. **Rabbi Akiva said to him: How will my** death come about? Rabbi Eliezer **said to him: Your** death will be **worse than theirs,** as you were my primary student and you did not come to study.

Rabbi Eliezer **raised his two arms and placed them on his heart,** and he **said: Woe to you, my two arms, as they are like two Torah scrolls that are** now **being rolled up,** and will never be opened again. **I have learned much Torah, and I have taught much Torah. I have learned much Torah, and I have not taken away from my teachers,** i.e., I have not received from their wisdom, **even like a dog lapping from the sea. I have taught much Torah, and my students have taken away from me,** i.e., they have received from my wisdom, **only like** the tiny amount that **a paintbrush** removes **from a tube** of paint.

Moreover, I can teach three hundred halakhot **with regard to a snow-white leprous mark** [bebaheret], **but no person has ever asked me anything about them.** He could not find a student who could fully understand him in those matters. **Moreover, I can teach three hundred** halakhot, **and some say** that Rabbi Eliezer said **three thousand** halakhot, **with regard to the planting of cucumbers** by sorcery, **but no person has ever asked me anything about them, besides Akiva ben Yosef.**

Rabbi Eliezer described the incident: **Once he and I were walking along the way,** and **he said to me: My teacher, teach me about the planting of cucumbers. I said one statement** of sorcery, and **the entire field became filled with cucumbers. He said to me: My teacher, you have taught me** about **planting them; teach me** about **uprooting them. I said one statement and they all were gathered to one place.**

The issue seems to be that the Rabbis were uncomfortable with *others* practicing magic, "[f]or [the Rabbis] it is only the Rabbi who is permitted to practice magic, while others, especially women, are forbidden, since the Rabbi's powers and purpose is derived from the sacred and women's powers are from another source, thought to be evil."[35]

---

35. Fishbane, Simcha. "'Most Women Engage in Sorcery'," p. 81.

Let us examine another case of Rabbi Eliezer's association with magic in the famous story of the oven of *akhnai*, which is a story that has to do with ritual purity or impurity of an oven shaped like a snake, but is used by the Rabbis to establish broader themes around the nature of Jewish law. It is often read as a story to establish the legal authority of the Rabbis and their disassociation with supernatural religion. In the story, the Rabbis do not listen to the voice of God and instead rely on logical reasoning and voting to establish the *halakhah* (law). I want to read the story from a different point of view through the lens of Rabbi Eliezer's association with magic. Rabbi Eliezer uses supernatural acts to appeal to his legal position.

The story occurs in a rabbinic setting where there is debate around a legal position and the Rabbis must decide what the *halakhah* is, i.e. what Jews would be expected to do in this particular situation. Rabbi Eliezer disagreed with the majority of the Sages with regard to their decision about the impurity of the oven of *akhnai*. Typically, the *halakhah* follows the majority, as the Rabbis read the statement "follow the multitude" (Exodus 23:2) to mean that a majority vote would establish legal precedent (Berakhot 9a). This was necessary to avoid a proliferation of legal options (Sanhedrin 22a). The principle was so sacrosanct that not even a heavenly voice (*bat kol*) could override the majority (Bava Metzia 59a).

However, Rabbi Eliezer proceeds to attempt to convince the Rabbis through his manipulation of natural phenomena. First, he causes a carob tree to be uprooted from its place. Then, he caused a stream of water to flow backwards, afterward causing the walls of the study hall to lean inward. With each case, the Rabbis reject his attempts to convince them with what is obviously magical practice and manipulation of nature.

Rabbi Eliezer then pulls out the big guns, calling on heaven to solve the dispute. A divine voice emerges and asks the Rabbis why they are not following the opinion of Rabbi Eliezer. They point to the verse in Deuteronomy which states that "it is not in heaven" (30:12), meaning the Torah, and that it is not decided through magic or prophecy but through logical deliberation and consensus-building.

This episode has immense personal consequences for Rabbi Eliezer. The Rabbis later burned everything he deemed pure and ostracized him from their group.

Bava Metzia 59b
 And this is known as **the oven of** akhnai. The Gemara asks: **What** is the relevance of akhnai, a snake, in this context? **Rav**

Yehuda said that **Shmuel said:** It is characterized in that manner due to the fact **that** the Rabbis **surrounded** it **with** their **statements like this snake,** which often forms a coil when at rest, **and deemed it impure.** The Sages **taught: On that day,** when they discussed this matter, **Rabbi Eliezer answered all** possible **answers in the world** to support his opinion, **but** the Rabbis **did not accept** his explanations **from him.**

After failing to convince the Rabbis logically, Rabbi Eliezer **said to them: If** the halakha is **in accordance with my** opinion, **this carob** tree **will prove** it. **The carob** tree **was uprooted from its place one hundred cubits, and some say four hundred cubits.** The Rabbis **said to him: One does not cite** halakhic **proof from the carob** tree. Rabbi Eliezer **then said to them: If** the halakha is **in accordance with my** opinion, **the stream will prove** it. The water in **the stream turned backward** and began flowing in the opposite direction. **They said to him: One does not cite** halakhic **proof from a stream.**

Rabbi Eliezer **then said to them: If** the halakha is **in accordance with my** opinion, **the walls of the study hall will prove** it. **The walls of the study hall leaned** inward and began **to fall. Rabbi Yehoshua scolded** the walls and **said to them: If Torah scholars are contending** with **each other in** matters of halakha, **what** is the **nature** of **your** involvement in this dispute? The Gemara relates: The walls **did not fall because of the deference** due **Rabbi Yehoshua, but they did not straighten because of** the **deference** due **Rabbi Eliezer, and they still remain leaning.**

Rabbi Eliezer **then said to them: If** the halakha is **in accordance with my** opinion, **Heaven will prove** it. **A Divine Voice emerged** from Heaven **and said: Why are you** differing **with Rabbi Eliezer, as** the halakha is **in accordance with** his opinion **in every place** that he expresses an opinion?

Rabbi Yehoshua stood on his feet and said: It is written: **"It is not in heaven"** (Deuteronomy 30:12). The Gemara asks: **What** is the relevance of the phrase **"It is not in heaven"** in this context? **Rabbi Yirmeya says:** Since **the Torah was already given at Mount Sinai, we do not regard a Divine Voice, as You already wrote at Mount Sinai, in the Torah: "After a majority to incline"** (Exodus 23:2). Since the majority of Rabbis disagreed with Rabbi Eliezer's opinion, the *halakha* is not ruled in accordance with his opinion. The Gemara relates: Years after, **Rabbi Natan encountered Elijah** the prophet and **said to him: What did the Holy One, Blessed be He, do at that time,** when Rabbi Yehoshua issued his declaration? Elijah **said to him:** The Holy One, Blessed be He, **smiled and**

said: My children have triumphed over Me; My children have triumphed over Me.

The Sages **said: On that day,** the Sages **brought all the ritually pure** items **deemed pure by** the ruling of **Rabbi Eliezer** with regard to the oven **and burned them in fire, and** the Sages **reached a consensus in his regard and ostracized him. And** the Sages **said: Who will go and inform him** of his ostracism? **Rabbi Akiva,** his beloved disciple, **said to them: I will go, lest an unseemly person go** and inform him in a callous and offensive manner, **and he would thereby destroy the entire world.**

What did Rabbi Akiva do? He wore black and wrapped himself in black, as an expression of mourning and pain, **and sat before** Rabbi Eliezer **at a distance of four cubits,** which is the distance that one must maintain from an ostracized individual. **Rabbi Eliezer said to him: Akiva, what** is different about **today from other days,** that you comport yourself in this manner? Rabbi Akiva **said to him: My teacher, it appears to me that your colleagues are distancing** themselves **from you.** He employed euphemism, as actually they distanced Rabbi Eliezer from them. Rabbi Eliezer **too, rent his garments and removed his shoes,** as is the custom of an ostracized person, **and he dropped** from his seat **and sat upon the ground.**

We will see Rabbi Eliezer again in our story, as he continually pops up throughout the rabbinic record around Jesus. This story proves his proximity to magical practice and going against the Rabbis' semi-rationalistic way of deciding law. In general, it shows the Rabbis' discomfort with overtly magical practice and their desire to distance themselves from such obvious practice of magic in religion.

The Rabbis' attitudes towards magic shows the place of magic in Jewish society at the time, given that the Rabbis were not willing to completely forbid it. Jewish magicians were well-renowned in the ancient world, "the repute of Jewish magicians exceeded even that of Egyptian sorcerers.[36]" The world of magic was highly syncretistic, as found in the Greek Magical Papyri, where one can find prayers to all sorts of pagan gods, but also to the "Lord of Hosts"[37], references to the angels Michael, Raphael, etc. and

36. Brashear, "The Greek Magical Papyri," p. 3426.

37. Schäfer, *Jesus in the Talmud*, p. 57–8, "In Jewish sources, it is above all the figure of the man-angel Enoch- Metatron, who is conspicuous for his close relationship with God through the power of his name. The antediluvian hero Enoch, who according to the Hebrew Bible did not die but was taken up into heaven (Gen. 5:24: "Enoch walked with God; then he was no more, for God took him"), was in fact—as the Third (Hebrew) Book

other reliance on Jewish names of God for magical purposes.[38] Scholars have found Jewish magical papyri, as well as incantation bowls, showing the prevalence of Jewish magic.[39]

Just as magic was undoubtedly commonplace in the ancient world, so was Gnosticism a series of speculative, philosophical and ritual mysticism that many practiced in Antiquity. It is found in Christian, Jewish, and pagan forms. Here I want to focus on the specifically Jewish version of Gnosticism as it pertains to the life of Jesus the Nazarene. I believe a central issue in his charge by the Sanhedrin relates to an issue of disputed Gnosticism and I have turned to the Jewish Encyclopedia to present the basics of gnosticism.

First, it must be noted that magic and Gnosticism go hand-in-hand, as magic is an important part of the doctrines and practice of Jewish Gnosticism. One of the key elements of Gnosticism is a speculative nature to understanding the Creation of the world and the heavenly throne-chariot (Ezekiel) as the dwelling of God. The rabbinic literature displays a cautious attitude toward discussion of the throne-chariot in Ezekiel. However, they were not opposed to studying it, only specifying that one must be a member of the rabbinic circle to do so (Ḥagigah 13a).

> Ḥagigah 2:1
>
> **One may not expound** the topic of **forbidden sexual relations before three** or more individuals; **nor** may one expound the **act of Creation** and the secrets of the beginning of the world **before two** or more individuals; **nor** may one expound **by oneself the** Design of the Divine **Chariot,** a mystical teaching with regard to the ways God conducts the world, **unless** he is **wise and understands** most matters **on his own.** The mishna continues in the same vein: **Whoever looks at four matters, it would have been better for him had he never entered the world:** Anyone who reflects upon **what** is **above** the firmament and **what is below** the earth, **what was before** Creation, **and what** will be **after** the end of

of Enoch, one of the texts of Merkava mysticism, explains—physically transformed into the highest angel Metatron, seated on a throne similar to God's throne of Glory, clothed in a majestic robe, crowned with a kingly crown, and called "The lesser YHWH" (*YHWH ha-qatan*), as it is written: "Since my name is in him" (Ex. 23:21).40 This verse refers to the angel of the Lord,41 who is identical with God because God's name is in him, that is, because he bears God's name. Whereas in the Bible the "angel of the Lord" is in- deed God himself, Metatron in 3 Enoch becomes the highest being next to God, due to the power of God's name residing in his name.

38. Alexander, "Incantations and Books of Magic," pp. 357–359.

39. Brashear, "The Greek Magical Papyri," p. 3428.

the world. **And anyone who has no concern for the honor of his Maker,** who inquires into and deals with matters not permitted to him, **deserves to have never come to the world.**

Gnosticism was a secret science that one needed to master after being initiated into a Gnostic group. Because Gnosticism gave one a secret key to understand the world and creation, it was considered dangerous for the uninitiated. As the Talmud notes:

Ḥagigah 13a
The Sages taught: An incident occurred **involving a youth who was reading the book of Ezekiel in the house of his teacher, and** he **was** able to **comprehend the electrum, and fire came out of the electrum and burned him. And they sought to suppress the book of Ezekiel** due to the danger it posed. **Ḥananya ben Ḥizkiya said to them: If this** youth happened to be **wise,** are **all** people **wise** enough to understand this book?

The youth here was "wise" meaning that he "knew", i.e. had gnosis.

It is important to note that Gnosticism was neither religion nor philosophy, but a combination of the two, especially given how these terms had different connotations in the ancient world. In fact, it was a fusion of philosophy, religion and magic with the latter taking a dominant role in its practice. Magic was connected with various symbols, tools, amulets, and the like, and the Jewish Encyclopedia gives a few examples of magic practices:

Jewish Encyclopedia
The following passage occurs in the Berlin Papyrus, 1:20, Parthey: "Take milk and honey and taste them, and something divine will be in your heart." The Talmud, curiously enough (Ḥagigah 13a), refers the phrase, "Honey and milk are under thy tongue" (Canticles 4:11), to the Merkabah, one of the principal parts of Jewish gnosis, saying that the knowledge of the Merkabah, which is sweeter than milk and honey, shall remain under the tongue, meaning that it shall not be taught ... The Valentinians taught that in order to attain salvation the pneumatic required nothing further "than gnosis and the formulæ of the mysteries" (Epiphanius, *Hæreses*, 31:7).

The language of "mysteries" is found in the New Testament and is a common name for the sacraments among the Eastern branches of Christianity. Related to the story of the Merkavah is a story found in rabbinic literature, here presented from the Tosefta, but also found in the Talmud (Ḥagigah 14b).

> *Tosefta Ḥagigah 2:2*[40]
>
> Four entered the orchard: Ben Azzai, Ben Zoma, another, and Rabbi Akiva. One looked and died. One looked and was harmed. One looked and cut down the trees. And one went up in peace and went down in peace. Ben Azzai looked and died. Scripture says about him (Psalms 116:15): "Precious in the sight of the LORD Is the death of His saints". Ben Zoma looked and was harmed. Scripture says about him (Proverbs 25:16): "Have you found honey? eat so much as is sufficient for you" and the continuation. [Cont. of the verse: "Lest thou be filled therewith, and vomit it." Elisha looked and cut down the trees. Scripture says about him (Ecclesiastes 5:5): "Suffer not your mouth to bring your flesh into guilt" etc. Rabbi Akiva went up in peace and went down in peace. Scripture says about him (Song of Songs 1:4): "Draw me, we will run after you" etc. They gave a parable: What is this similar to? To the orchard of a king and there is an attic above it. It is upon [the man] to look so long as he does not move [his eyes] from it. Another parable was given. What is this similar to? To [a street] that passes between two paths, one of fire, and one of snow. If it leans one way, it gets burned [by the fire]. If it leans the other way it gets burned by the snow. A man must walk in the middle and not lean to or fro. A story of Rabbi Yehoshua [Who was walking in the street and Ben Zoma came opposite him] he reached him and did not greet him. He said to him [from where and to where] Ben Zoma? He said to him: I was watching the creation, and there is not between the upper waters and the lower waters even a handbreadth. As it is written (Genesis 1:2) "and the spirit of God hovered over the face of the waters". And it says (Deuteronomy 32:11): "As a vulture that stirs up her nest" etc. Just as the vulture flies over the nest, touching and not touching, so too there is not even a handbreadth between the upper waters and lower waters. Rabbi Yehoshua said to his students: Ben Zoma is already outside. In a few days, Ben Zoma passed away.

There is a connection to Gnosticism here found in the writings of Philo:

> *Philo, De Allegoriis Legum," §§ 52 et seq.; ed. Mangey, §§ 117 et seq.*

---

40. Archaic language in the original translation was modernized.

> Philo says, similarly: "Some one might ask, 'If true holiness consists in imitating the deeds of God, why should I be forbidden to plant a grove in the sanctuary of God, since God did the same thing when He planted a garden?' . . . While God plants and sows the beautiful in the soul, the spirit sins, saying, 'I plant '"

It seems that gnosis was discussed using the metaphor of planting trees. For Philo, the mystic/Gnostic imitates God and becomes a creator of sorts, planting a tree, in knowing the mysteries of creation.

Jewish gnosticism shared with its non-Jewish varieties a form of dualism. This is because the gnostics regarded the physical realm as somehow bad, with all Gnostic groups sharing the idea that the physical world was evil or tainted and that God could not have been involved with creating the evil material world. For some Gnostics this implied a "good" God and a "bad" God. Some Christian Gnostics even went so far as to say that the God of the Old Testament was the Demiurge, the evil creator God, and that Jesus had been sent by the good God to provide an escape from the evil of materiality.

Judaism and Jewish Gnostics did not fully believe in the doctrine of the Demiurge. However, there was an idea called the "two powers" (*shete reshuyot*), which contrasted with the official view in the Tanakh. God created the world by his word, "By the word of the LORD the heavens were made, by the breath of His mouth, all their host . . . For He spoke, and it was; He commanded, and it endured (Psalm 33:6, 9). There are other traditions in the official narrative that might hint towards a Gnostic understanding. The Jerusalem Targum translates "He spoke" referring to God as "he willed". The Torah was thought to have existed two thousand years before creation (Genesis Rabbah 8:2) and the Jerusalem Targum adds an interesting insight into the following biblical passage:

Genesis 1:26
And God said, "Let us make humankind in our image, after our likeness. They shall rule the fish of the sea, the birds of the sky, the cattle, the whole earth, and all the creeping things that creep on earth."

Jerusalem Targum
And the <u>Word of the Lord</u> created man in His likeness, in the likeness of the presence of the Lord He created him, the male and his yoke-fellow He created them.

The Torah was an instrument of creation in Bereishit Rabbah 1. All of this points to a simple conclusion: that some form of gnosis is acceptable in rabbinic Judaism. Several Rabbis are described as participating in some way in Gnostic circles. Aḥer (Elisha ben Abuyah) seems to have been a critic of Jewish morality (Pesaḥim 56a), according to the Jewish Encyclopedia. There also, Rabbi Jose ben Ḥalafta is regarded as a Gnostic for the saying attributed to him "five plants that he planted" which is the language of gnosis.

Elisha ben Abuyah leads us to a figure in Jewish Gnosticism: the Metatron. This is a prominent angel in the heavenly court and part of Jewish angelology. Metatron is a figure of some importance in later Kabbalah as well as in earlier Gnostic texts. It is an angel, often conceived of in dualistic terms with God.

The Talmud includes a story about Elisha ben Abuya and the Metatron. It is after he became a heretic, chopping "down the saplings" returning to the tree metaphors associated with Gnosticism He was led to heresy *because he saw Metatron*. His heresy was to say that there were "two powers" or authorities, i.e. dualism. The Rabbis banish Aher and scold Metatron for this incident.

> *Ḥagigah 15a*
>
> The Gemara stated earlier that Aḥer **chopped down the saplings,** becoming a heretic. **With regard to him, the verse states: "Do not let your mouth bring your flesh into guilt"** (Ecclesiastes 5:5). The Gemara poses a question: **What was** it that led him to heresy? **He saw** the angel **Mitatron, who was granted permission to sit and write the merits** of Israel. He said: There is **a tradition** that in the world **above there is no sitting; no competition; no** turning one's **back before Him,** i.e., all face the Divine Presence; **and no lethargy.** Seeing that someone other than God was seated above, **he said: Perhaps,** the Gemara here interjects, **Heaven forbid, there are two authorities,** and there is another source of power in control of the world in addition to God. Such thoughts led *Aḥer* to heresy.
>
> The Gemara relates: **They removed Mitatron** from his place in heaven **and smote him** with **sixty rods** [pulsei] **of fire,** so that others would not make the mistake that *Aḥer* made. **They said** to the angel: **What is the reason** that **when you saw** Elisha ben Avuya **you did not stand before him?** Despite this conduct, since Mitatron was personally involved, he **was granted permission to erase the merits of** Aḥer and cause him to stumble in any manner.

> A Divine Voice went forth saying: "Return, rebellious children"
> (Jeremiah 3:22), **apart from** Aḥer.
>
> Upon hearing this, Elisha ben Avuya **said: Since that man,**
> meaning himself, **has been banished from that world, let him go**
> **out and enjoy this world.** Aḥer **went astray.** He went and **found a**
> **prostitute** and **solicited her** for intercourse. **She said to him: And**
> are **you not Elisha ben Avuya?** Shall a person of your stature per-
> form such an act? **He uprooted a radish from a patch** of radishes
> **on Shabbat and gave it to her,** to demonstrate that he no longer
> observed the Torah. The prostitute **said: He is other** than he was.
> He is not the same Elisha ben Avuya, he is *Aḥer*, other.

The nature of Aher's heresy is his dualism. In fact, heresy throughout the Talmud is associated with a belief in "two powers" or dualism, which they generally prohibit.

> *Ḥullin 87a*
>
> **Come** and **hear** a proof from an incident in **which a certain**
> **heretic said to Rabbi** Yehuda HaNasi: **He who created moun-**
> **tains did not create wind, and he who created wind did not**
> **create mountains;** rather, each was created by a separate deity, **as**
> **it is written: "For behold, He Who forms the mountains and**
> **He Who creates the wind"** (Amos 4:13), indicating that there are
> two deities: One who forms the mountains and one who creates
> the wind. Rabbi Yehuda HaNasi **said to him: Imbecile, go to the**
> **end of the verse,** which states: **"The Lord, the God of hosts, is**
> **His name."** The verse emphasizes that God is the One Who both
> forms and creates.

In another incident, the Rabbis deal with a heretic who interprets a reference to "Lord" in Exodus 24:1 as referring to Metatron, which is derived from the angel "sent before you" in Exodus 23:20–21. The heretic believed that Metatron should be worshiped. The Rabbis quickly refute this idea, as one would expect.

> *Sanhedrin 38b*
>
> **A certain heretic said to Rav Idit: It is written** in the verse
> concerning God: **"And to Moses He said: up to the Lord"** (Exodus
> 24:1). The heretic raised a question: **It should have** stated: **Come**
> **up to Me.** Rav Idit **said to him: This** term, "the Lord," in that verse
> **is** referring to the angel **Metatron, whose name is like the name**
> **of his Master,** as it is written: "Behold I send an angel before you
> to keep you in the way and to bring you to the place that I have
> prepared. Take heed of him and obey his voice; do not defy him;

71

for he will not pardon your transgression, **for My name is in him"**
(Exodus 23:20–21).

The heretic said to him: **If so,** if this angel is equated with
God, **we should worship him** as we worship God. Rav Idit said
to him: It **is written: "Do not defy** [tammer] **him,"** which alludes
to: **Do not replace Me** [temireni] **with him.** The heretic said to
him: **If so, why do** I need the clause **"For he will not pardon your
transgression"?** Rav Idit **said to him: We believe that we did not
accept** the angel **even as a guide** [befarvanka] for the journey, **as
it is written: "And he said to him: If Your Presence go not with
me** raise us not up from here" (Exodus 33:15).

The important piece of information to derive from this is that heresy was equated with dualism and the belief in two powers or dualism in
Metatron. Some even divinized Metatron and worshiped him. Christianity
is the main source of heresy for the early Rabbis, and in this we can see the
nascent Christology as Jesus was identified with Metatron and made into
a deity.

The concept of "two powers" can be understood as a contrast between
the manifestation of deity (theophany) which is represented by God and
the second power's epiphany in Metatron (meaning a manifestation of a
lesser divine being). In the Jewish tradition, God is attributed with qualities
related to the voice, i.e. God always *speaks*, whereas the lesser power *appears*
as a great angel. We thus have the contrast between the vision of Metatron
and the voice of God, which is developed throughout biblical and Jewish
history. It is well known that, in the Bible, God appears and is described in
anthropomorphic terms. This explains the idea that God created human-
ity *in his image* (Genesis 1:27), meaning that God was originally viewed
as having a body as we do, and explains the plethora of body-like images
applied to God throughout the Bible. There is also a counter-narrative in
the biblical text, which is where what Orlov calls the "aural symbolism"
originates, in the Deuteronomistic school and later prophetic tradition.[41]

It was the Deuteronomistic school that (eventually) won out in rabbinic circles. Returning to a *sugya* in the Gemara, in Ḥagigah 15a, we see
Metatron, envisioned with human features, as he "sits" and "writes" the
merits of Israel. Yet, throughout the Talmud, God is depicted in aural symbolism through his divine voice. Any anthropomorphic language used to
describe God in the rabbinic tradition was eventually faded out by the medieval ages, when the great philosopher, Moses Maimonides, cemented the

---

41. Orlov, Andrei A.. "Two Powers in Heaven

Jewish opposition to anthropomorphism by representing a larger school of thought within Andalusian Judaism that read these as metaphors in the biblical text.

We learn about Jesus' association with magic in the context of writing on Shabbat. We do learn one new detail of Jesus' life in this *sugya*, "Didn't the infamous ben Stada take magic spells out of Egypt in a scratch on his flesh?" The Rabbis associated Jesus with Egypt, just as the Gospels, but as the means when he learned magic spells (later one of the charges presented against him in his trial). The sentence serves a legal purpose, "They said to him: He was a fool, and you cannot cite proof from a fool," talking about legal precedent. The interesting thing about the Talmudic narratives, in my point of view, is the conversational way they are presented. It is as if we could imagine the Rabbis sitting around a table and saying, "Oh, didn't old Ben Stada go to Egypt to practice idolatry?" I have no doubt that there were rumors, legends, gossip, etc. that circulated about Jesus that was passed down. Perhaps, even maybe, but probably not, the Rabbis had some sort of alternative history that should be taken into account.

> *Shabbat 104b*
> If **one** unwittingly **scratches** letters **on his flesh** on Shabbat, Rabbi Eliezer deems him liable to bring a sin-offering and the Sages deem him exempt. **It was taught** in a *baraita* that **Rabbi Eliezer said to the Rabbis: Didn't** the infamous **ben Stada take magic spells out of Egypt in a scratch on his flesh? They said to him: He was a fool, and you cannot cite proof from a fool.**

Jesus was remembered as a *magician* by the Rabbis – someone who practiced magic in a way that was prohibited by the Rabbis. We saw that the Rabbis were not so innocent of the practice of magic themselves but did draw some lines around the practice. Later, we will see that Jesus' teaching in the Talmud *seems* to be associated with some Gnostic ideas, leading to my assertion that he was some form of early Gnostic, as those ideas pre-dated first-century Christianity.

THE NASARAEANS

The Nasaraeans were a Jewish sect that lived in the Transjordan in Gilead and Bashan in modern-day Jordan. Epiphanius goes to great lengths to distinguish the "Nasaraeans" from the Nazoraeans, a later group, and that the latter never called themselves Nasaraioi (Nasaraeans). Unfortunately,

Epiphanius is not the most reliable historian and can only be relied upon reluctantly. However, his insistence on the distinction between the Nasaraeans and Nazoraeans begs the question as to why he is so adamant that these two seemingly related groups were nothing at all alike.

The name might come from the references in the Old Testament to *migdal notsrim*, "watchtowers" (2 Kings 17:9). The root is used in other contexts in the Tanakh to refer to keeping the law and its statutes.[42] The Nasaraeans must have seen themselves as faithful keepers of the genuine Law of Moses.

They practiced what Epiphanius considered to be normative Judaism, with few distinctive beliefs (*Panarion* 18 1:1). They existed before Christ and did not know him (*Panarion* 29 6:1) and were grouped with the pre-Christian heresies. Other examples of this include the Hemerobaptists, Oceans and Esseans. He remarks that they observed the Sabbath and circumcised their sons, as they would as observant Jews, but "did not inculcate fate or astrology" (*Panarion* 18 1:2), noting that they observed *the same Sabbath and observed the same festivals.*

They recognized many of the *characters* from the Torah, including Adam, Seth, Enoch, Methuselah, Noah, Abraham, Isaac, Jacob, Levi, and Aaron, Moses, and Joshua (*Panarion* 18 3:1), acknowledging that Moses had received legislation but that legislation was not the Torah. This has some parallel in Mandean teaching, where the Jews are said to falsify the Law (*Ginza* 43:21–23).

The Nasaraeans rejected sacrifice and eating meat, "though they were Jews who kept all the Jewish observances, they would not offer sacrifice or eat meat; in their eyes it was unlawful to eat meat or make sacrifices with it. They claimed that these books are forgeries and that none of these customs were instituted by the fathers" (*Panarion* 18 1:4). They also claimed that any text showing support for these practices were forgeries and not instituted by God (*Panarion* 18 1:4).

Epiphanius was somewhat confused by the Nasaraeans' position, questioning their acceptance of Moses but not the Law, "Since no other writing speaks of them, how do they know the fathers' names and excellence if not from the Pentateuchal writings themselves?" (*Panarion* 18 2:1). Epiphanius speaks against their views for a few sections before finishing the section on the Nasaraeans.

42. Deuteronomy 33:9; Psalms 25:10

What do we make of Epiphanius' claims about the Nasaraeans? As stated earlier, the reluctance to create any suspicion of association between the groups leads to question Epiphanius' motives here. There have been few scholarly treatments of this group. However, earlier works make mention of them. The Nasaraeans have been compared with the Rechabites and Kenites in the Hebrew Bible (1 Chronicles 2:55)[43], who were descendants of Jethro, Moses' father-in-law. The prophet "took some Rechabites into the Temple and offered them wine to drink, and that they declined on the ground that Jehonadab, son of Rechab, their ancestor, had commanded them not to drink wine or other strong drink, or to live in houses, or to sow seed, or to plant vineyards, and had enjoined them to dwell in tents all their days" (Jewish Encyclopedia). The Jewish Encyclopedia continues:

> God's promise that the Rechabites "shall not want a man to stand before me forever" (Jer. 35:19) is interpreted by R. Jonathan to mean that they shall become scribes and members of the Sanhedrin. Other rabbis say the Rechabites married their daughters to priests and had grandchildren in the priesthood (Yalkut Jeremiah 323). Jonathan's appears to be the accepted view, as the Rechabites became scribes (I Chronicles 2:55) and sat with the Sanhedrin in the granite chamber ("lishkat ha-gazit"; perhaps the same as the chamber of Hanan) of the Temple. The names of the subdivided families, the Tirathites, the Shemeathites, and the Suchathites (*ib.*), are appellations indicating their learning and (in the case of the last-named) their custom of living in tents (Mek., Yitro, 2:60b; Sifre, Num. 78 [ed. Friedmann, p. 20a]; Sotah 11a). R, Nathan remarked that God's covenant with the Rechabites was superior to the covenant with David, inasmuch as David's was conditional (Ps. 132:12), while that with the Rechabites was without reservation (Mek., *l.c.*). The Talmud identifies "ha-yoẓerim" ("the potters"; I Chronicles 4:23) as the Rechabites, because they observed ("she-naẓeru") the commandment of their father (Bava Batra 91b). Evidently the Talmud had the reading "ha-noẓerim" (="diligent observers") instead of "ha-yoẓerim." This would explain the term "Migdal Noẓerim," the habitation of the Rechabites, in contrast with a "fenced city" (II Kings 17:9, 18:8). The appellation of "Notzerim" or "Notzerites" is perhaps changed from "Nazarites" as indicative of the temperate life of the Rechabites.

The location of the Rechabites around the lake of Merom is not far from the places mentioned by Epiphanius where the Nasaraeans lived in

---

43. Kampmeier, A. The Pre-Christian Nasareans.

Gilead and Bashan. The Rechabites seemed to have their own alternative laws, likely claiming that the Mosaic law was a falsification of the true law. Kampmeier notes, "The fact stands out that the legislation as represented in the Pentateuch was never accepted during Hebrew history by all Israelites, though they were one in the worship of the national Yahveh, of which in recent years we again have received a proof through the discoveries in Elephantine, and the Nasareans of Epiphanius seem to have belonged to those protesting against the Pentateuch."[44]

Kampmeier also mentions that the ideas associated with the Nasaraeans were not as uncommon as previously thought. The Essenes might have had vegetarian diets and had reservations about the Temple system. Josephus' own teacher engaged in a vegetarian-style lifestyle and asceticism. Josephus describes Banus as such, "lived in the desert, used no other clothing than grew upon trees, had no other food than what grew of its own accord, and bathed himself in cold water frequently, both by night and by day, in order to preserve his chastity. I imitated him in those things, and continued with him three years."[45]

They must have been the first group to reject animal sacrifices and tend towards vegetarianism, although they were not the first.

Did they accept Enoch, a sort of "alternative" Torah?

The mention of Enoch brings to mind the scholarly designation of "Enochic Judaism" which operated in the few centuries before the common area. The positions of Enochic Judaism, mostly notably associated with the Book of Enoch, include the following positions. First, it was "a unique concept of the origins of evil that made the 'fall angels' [Genesis 6:1–4]... as ultimately responsible for the spread of evil and impurity on earth."[46] They rejected other conceptualizations of God's order in the world and argued that it had been replaced by the disorder in the world. Besides their overtly cosmological orientation, they also held to a strong belief in the "end of days", a time of final judgment that would arrive soon. This would initiate a type of second creation, a new world that would correct the disorder. They also rejected the legitimacy of the ruling priesthood in Jerusalem. They attributed to Enoch characteristics of priesthood, making him an intercessor between God and the fallen angels. There might have been some pure pre-Aaronite priesthood but that was not the then current Zadokite

---

44. Kampmeier, A. The Pre-Christian Nasareans, p. 88

45. Josephus, *Life*, 2.

46. Boccaccini, *Roots*, p. 90.

priesthood. They were also well-known for their calendar, which differed from other Jewish calendars consisting of three hundred sixty-four days with a "seasonal cycle of two thirty-day and one thirty-one-day months."[47] Enochic Judaism seemed willing to re-read and give new meaning to older narratives, such as the story of the fallen angels in Genesis 6:1–4. Enochic Judaism arose during the Second Temple period, although it is difficult to pinpoint exact dates, as with most historical events. There were already calendrical discussions in the 3rd century BCE, presuming that some of these ideas might have already begun to take shape; Boccaccini places the beginning of the movement in the 4th century BCE. The movement seems to be an intra-priestly conflict with a group of priests and scribes who felt marginalized by the current order, although Hanson presented a case that this group might have been non-priestly. Boccaccini agrees that this was an intra-priestly conflict (p. 99). The rejection of this group of priests by the Zadokite leadership in Jerusalem was spiritualized to a conflict above between spiritual forces. However, this movement was not schismatic but the Maccabbean revolt would create the conditions to grow and cause the movement to begin to splinter from other Judaisms.

The question remains as to what the possible relationship between the Nasaraeans and the Enochic tradition might be. We have only fragmentary evidence and arriving at any conclusion is beyond satisfactory answering. However, we can postulate that there is *some* relationship between early Christianity and the Enochic tradition. This can be assumed due to the references and allusions to the book of Enoch in the New Testament (most famously in Jude 14–15, 1 Enoch 2:1–2, although in many other places). We can also presume that the Nasaraean sect was the ancestor of Nazarene Christianity. The clearest overlap in the traditions is the rejection of the priesthood, although this leads to different conclusions. It is also important to recall that the Nasaraean movement existed in the 1st century BCE, well during the time that Enochic Judaism had begun to spin off several descendant traditions. While we have no evidence that the Nasaraeans accepted the Enochic calendar, it is not impossible. It might even be possible that they accepted the book of Enoch and Jubilees as representing authentic Mosaic traditions and legislation.

There is also a possibility that the Nasaraeans might be connected with the modern Mandaeans. The milieu of Jewish sectarianism (including mainstream sects like the Sadducees and Pharisees) was likely more

47. Boccaccini, *Roots*, p. 93

diverse than we have imagined. Therefore, it should not seem so unlikely that there might have been smaller groups, perhaps like the Nasaraeans, that had *some* overlap with other groups, but also with their own distinctive beliefs and practices.

This mysterious group is unfortunately not well documented. However, its origins "before Christ", as Epiphanius describes, allows it to be considered as the possible sect of Jesus. Throughout the Talmud, Jesus is referred to as *ha notsri*, "the *Notsri.*" This root is related to the name of the Nasaraeans. It is my contention that Jesus was a member of this sect and the title *ha notsri* refers to his identification as a Nasaraean.

What Was Jesus' Lifestyle Like?

THE TALMUD REFERS TO Jesus as "close to the government" (*qarob la-malkhut*), which corresponds to aspects of Jesus' lifestyle through a reading of his habits as presented in the Christian Gospels.[1]

Everything we know about Jesus points to any other way of describing his social status. The Gospels describe him as a poor peasant, from Nazareth, which is in the middle of nowhere. He does not get along with the upper classes either . . . or so it seems. But what if the Gospels contained underlying clues about Jesus' social status? What if they revealed a man accustomed to luxury and wealth? Through a close reading of the Gospel we can find such clues, bearing in mind this statement of "close to the government" and in examining socio-cultural customs of the time.

The Talmud notes that those who are "close to the government" are not necessarily nice people. "They bore names and garments intended to frighten their victims, and had horses and mules parading before them. These men were in the habit of whipping their victims and would not hesitate to kill with impunity anyone that refused to comply."[2] This is to say that the Talmud and the Rabbis had a negative view of those "close to the government" and would only have assigned that label to Jesus if there were some kernel of truth to the statement. If we re-read some Gospel accounts of Jesus' life, we can see where they might have found this description to be true. Not that Jesus was going around killing people, but he does sometimes demonstrate an inhospitable attitude and has a quick temper.

---

1. This chapter was inspired by Faur, José. *The Gospel According to the Jews.*

2. Faur, *Gospel According to the Jews*, p. 113

Where do we see this in the life of Jesus? We know that Jesus loved good food and drink, "the Son of Man came eating and drinking, and they say, 'Look, a glutton and a drunkard, a friend of tax collectors and sinners!' Yet wisdom is vindicated by her deeds" (Matthew 11:19). Christians tend to understand this passage as showing the stubbornness of the Jewish people for not accepting Christ (in the preceding verses) and skip over the part about eating and drinking, except to show that Jesus was a "friend of sinners" because he came to bring redemption. Perhaps though, there is something negative about being associated with drunks, gluttons, tax collectors and sinners?

The dictum in Mark 7:15 reveals Jesus' proclivity for good food, even if it meant disregarding Jewish dietary laws, where it states, "there is nothing outside a person that by going in can defile, but the things that come out are what defile." This is the episode where Jesus (in Mark) "declares all foods clean." I believe this passage is more reflective of the Pauline groups and resonates well with Paul's dispense of the Torah for non-Jews. However, perhaps there is a trace of some historical memory here, although it does seem to clash with the Nazarene/Ebionite vision of Jesus as vegetarian.

There is a peculiar episode in the Gospel of Mark in which Jesus curses a fig tree for bearing no fruit, because Jesus was hungry. The only problem was that it was spring, and it was not the fig's fruit-bearing season. Christian commentaries tend to allegorize this story to refer to Israel. An online Christian commentary notes, "The tree was cursed for its *pretense* of leaves, not for its *lack* of fruit. Like Israel in the days of Jesus, it had the outward form but no fruit. In this picture, Jesus warned Israel—and us—of God's displeasure when we have the *appearance* of fruit but not the fruit itself. God is not pleased when His people are all leaves and no fruit" (Enduring Word Commentary[3]). It is certainly a far-fetched reading of the story. The last line gives it away "And his disciples heard it". Now why would the Gospel record that statement? Of course his disciples heard it! Perhaps it was reported in this way to reflect that they heard the words, but wondered why he would say that. Maybe Jesus was a bit upset that he was unable to find a snack.[4]

---

3. Available online: https://enduringword.com/bible-commentary/

4. This is Faur's somewhat facetious interpretation. As Dykstra, Tom. *Mark Canonizer of Paul* explains, "Considering the symbolism of the sea of Galilee in the rest of Mark and the location of this text surrounding the temple cleansing episode, it is no great leap to see the "mountain" as an allusion to the temple mount and the sea as the Roman sea.107 This view of the temple and its fate, as expressed metaphorically in the

Mark 11:13–14
On the following day, when they came from Bethany, he was hungry. Seeing in the distance a fig tree in leaf, he went to see whether perhaps he would find anything on it. When he came to it, he found nothing but leaves, for it was not the season for figs. He said to it, "May no one ever eat fruit from you again." And his disciples heard it.

We could also consider the episode on the Sabbath, where Jesus' disciples plucked grain to eat, in clear violation of Sabbath laws. It was permitted to pluck grains in another man's field, provided that no agricultural tools were used.

Deuteronomy 23:26
When you enter another man's field of standing grain, you may pluck ears with your hand; but you must not put a sickle to your neighbor's grain.

This could be *any* person's field (Bava Metzia 92a) but this is prohibited on the Sabbath (Shabbat 73b), making Jesus and his disciples liable for breaking the Sabbath laws. But Jesus and his disciples were hungry (Matthew 12:1). The Pharisees witness this (v. 2) and condemn him and his disciples. The Gospel of Matthew presents a type of *halakhic* defense, by referring to an episode in the life of David, "He said to them, "Have you not read what David did when he and his companions were hungry? He entered the house of God and ate the bread of the Presence, which it was not lawful for him or his companions to eat, but only for the priests. Or have you not read in the law that on the sabbath the priests in the temple break the sabbath and yet are guiltless?" (v. 3–5). Yet, David and his companions were *starving*, not hungry, as the original story shows. This text was not used in any rabbinic legal argumentation.

1 Samuel 21:1–7
David came to Nob to the priest Ahimelech. Ahimelech came trembling to meet David, and said to him, "Why are you alone, and no one with you?" David said to the priest Ahimelech, "The king has charged me with a matter, and said to me, 'No one must

---

fig tree parable and literally in the Isaiah quotation that concludes the temple cleansing, perfectly represents the understanding behind the Pauline mission. The physical temple in Jerusalem was of no importance to Paul; it had in a sense "withered away to its roots," being replaced by the "Jerusalem above" (Gal 4:25–26). This Jerusalem above was available to all, including the Gentiles, wherever they lived; thus "he house of prayer for all the nations" was metaphorically thrown into the Roman sea (p. 91).

know anything of the matter about which I send you, and with which I have charged you.' I have made an appointment with the young men for such and such a place. Now then, what have you at hand? Give me five loaves of bread, or whatever is here." The priest answered David, "I have no ordinary bread at hand, only holy bread—provided that the young men have kept themselves from women." David answered the priest, "Indeed women have been kept from us as always when I go on an expedition; the vessels of the young men are holy even when it is a common journey; how much more today will their vessels be holy?" So the priest gave him the holy bread; for there was no bread there except the bread of the Presence, which is removed from before the Lord, to be replaced by hot bread on the day it is taken away.

Jesus and his disciples disregarded public fast days, distinguishing themselves from the Pharisees and even John's disciples. In keeping with this theme, Jesus is accustomed to eating to his full and we have seen several cases where he goes to great lengths to satiate himself and his disciples. It makes sense, then, that he would be opposed to fasting. Christian commentators see this as a reference to the special time while Jesus was alive. However, it might reveal more about Jesus' attitude towards the Torah and its observance than the messianic era. The Gospel of Thomas records Jesus' opposition to fasting.[5]

> *Mark 12:18–20*
> Now John's disciples and the Pharisees were fasting; and people came and said to him, "Why do John's disciples and the disciples of the Pharisees fast, but your disciples do not fast?" Jesus said to them, "The wedding guests cannot fast while the bridegroom is with them, can they? As long as they have the bridegroom with them, they cannot fast. The days will come when the bridegroom is taken away from them, and then they will fast on that day.

One of the more fascinating aspects of this reading of the Gospels is his attention to the detail of Jesus' opposition to washing his hands before meals. Jesus is invited by a Pharisee to have dinner and immediately sits at his place and does not wash his hands. It is likely that Jesus expected to be attended to by a servant, noting his behavior in other similar contexts. When the Pharisee expresses amazement at Jesus' social behavior, Jesus launches into an attack on the Pharisees *as a group*, which shows a lack of social graces. Jesus must have been one awkward party guest!

5. Sayings 6, 14, 104

Luke 11:37–54

While he was speaking, a Pharisee invited him to dine with him; so he went in and took his place at the table. The Pharisee was amazed to see that he did not first wash before dinner. Then the Lord said to him, "Now you Pharisees clean the outside of the cup and of the dish, but inside you are full of greed and wickedness. You fools! Did not the one who made the outside make the inside also? So give for alms those things that are within; and see, everything will be clean for you.

"But woe to you Pharisees! For you tithe mint and rue and herbs of all kinds, and neglect justice and the love of God; it is these you ought to have practiced, without neglecting the others. Woe to you Pharisees! For you love to have the seat of honor in the synagogues and to be greeted with respect in the marketplaces. Woe to you! For you are like unmarked graves, and people walk over them without realizing it."

One of the lawyers answered him, "Teacher, when you say these things, you insult us too." And he said, "Woe also to you lawyers! For you load people with burdens hard to bear, and you yourselves do not lift a finger to ease them. Woe to you! For you build the tombs of the prophets whom your ancestors killed. So you are witnesses and approve of the deeds of your ancestors; for they killed them, and you build their tombs. Therefore also the Wisdom of God said, 'I will send them prophets and apostles, some of whom they will kill and persecute,' so that this generation may be charged with the blood of all the prophets shed since the foundation of the world, from the blood of Abel to the blood of Zechariah, who perished between the altar and the sanctuary. Yes, I tell you, it will be charged against this generation. Woe to you lawyers! For you have taken away the key of knowledge; you did not enter yourselves, and you hindered those who were entering."

When he went outside, the scribes and the Pharisees began to be very hostile toward him and to cross-examine him about many things, lying in wait for him, to catch him in something he might say.

The Gospel author presents this and blames the Pharisees and scribes (called lawyers too, who were also cursed by Jesus) as they "began to be very hostile toward him" – with good reason. How would you respond if you invited someone to dinner and they expected you to wash their feet and didn't wash their hands? What if they then insulted *you* after you made that observation? I would probably be hostile toward him as well!

Mark presents a story of Jesus' disciples interacting with the Pharisees, who note that the disciples did not wash their hands, "according to the tradition of the elders". It is hard to know exactly what this refers to because it could refer to an early form of ritual hand washing (*netilat yadayim*) that perhaps Judeo-Christians opposed. However, this can be read as referring to normal hand washing. Jesus again launches into a dispute with the Pharisees about the nature of their traditions, again showing his short temper.

> *Mark 7:1–5*
> Now when the Pharisees and some of the scribes who had come from Jerusalem gathered around him, they noticed that some of his disciples were eating with defiled hands, that is, without washing them. (For the Pharisees, and all the Jews, do not eat unless they thoroughly wash their hands, thus observing the tradition of the elders; and they do not eat anything from the market unless they wash it; and there are also many other traditions that they observe, the washing of cups, pots, and bronze kettles.) So the Pharisees and the scribes asked him, "Why do your disciples not live according to the tradition of the elders, but eat with defiled hands?"

These episodes show that Jesus had a lack of etiquette in many situations, a short temper, and was from a certain social class (which we will explore in detail below). The book of Proverbs exhorts one to behave politely as a guest in another's home (Proverbs 17:13), a trait that Jesus appears to have lacked. The statement "it is what comes out of the mouth that defiles a man" (Matt. 15:11) could be seen as ironic, considering other aspects of Jesus' behavior in the Gospels.

Before continuing, I think it is important to note that these behaviors do not necessarily disqualify Jesus as a teacher, but they do humanize him. I think that makes him more relatable, as we see the things that upset him, a bit about his social circles and upbringing and his limitations as a man. It is also quite possible that we are seeing Jesus' passion for his own religious ideas. The previous episodes show Jesus' opposition to fasting and handwashing, perhaps referring to the ritual observed by the Pharisees and later rabbinic Judaism. Perhaps Jesus was so passionate about his ideas and interpretation of Torah to disregard social etiquette when confronting a practice with which he disagreed.[6]

---

6. See the next chapter for a further discussion of Jesus' beliefs.

In contrast to his aversion to washing his hands, Jesus enjoyed having his feet washed with expensive oil, a story found in several of the Gospels. In John 12:1–6, Jesus even allows for an oil worth 300 denarii to be used to massage his feet, recalling that a worker earned one denarius a day (Matthew 20:2–13). In this story in Luke, Jesus is again dining with a Pharisee and takes his place at the table. A woman "who was a sinner" then came and brought a jar of expensive ointment.; she touched his feet, cleaning them, kissing them and anointing them with the ointment. Now, this is certainly in breach of rabbinic codes of morality between men and women and appropriate touch. The Pharisee, named Simon, questions Jesus' behavior. Jesus, of course, responds with a condemnation and a story, although he seems less angry in this episode. Towards the end, he addresses Simon, "Do you see this woman? I entered your house; you gave me no water for my feet, but she has bathed my feet with her tears and dried them with her hair. You gave me no kiss, but from the time I came in she has not stopped kissing my feet. You did not anoint my head with oil, but she has anointed my feet with ointment (v. 44–46). Jesus *expected* his feet to be washed and, for that reason, took pity on this woman (often assumed to be a prostitute) and goes so far as to proclaim that her sins were forgiven. In context, it seems like hyperbole, rather than divine pronouncement.

> *Luke 7:36–39*
> One of the Pharisees asked Jesus to eat with him, and he went into the Pharisee's house and took his place at the table. And a woman in the city, who was a sinner, having learned that he was eating in the Pharisee's house, brought an alabaster jar of ointment. She stood behind him at his feet, weeping, and began to bathe his feet with her tears and to dry them with her hair. Then she continued kissing his feet and anointing them with the ointment. Now when the Pharisee who had invited him saw it, he said to himself, "If this man were a prophet, he would have known who and what kind of woman this is who is touching him—that she is a sinner."

Another story which is often read in Christian circles to show the humility of a woman anointing Jesus' feet read in context seems to show Jesus' luxurious lifestyle. In this story, some who were with him question if such expensive oil could have been used more wisely, perhaps to help the poor. Jesus responds that the poor will always be with them, but he will not, implying that honoring him is more important than helping the poor.

> *Mark 14:3–8*

> While he was at Bethany in the house of Simon the leper, as he sat at the table, a woman came with an alabaster jar of very costly ointment of nard, and she broke open the jar and poured the ointment on his head. But some were there who said to one another in anger, "Why was the ointment wasted in this way? For this ointment could have been sold for more than three hundred denarii, and the money given to the poor." And they scolded her. But Jesus said, "Let her alone; why do you trouble her? She has performed a good service for me. For you always have the poor with you, and you can show kindness to them whenever you wish; but you will not always have me. She has done what she could; she has anointed my body beforehand for its burial.

Jesus always "reclined" when he ate and chastised hosts when they did not wash his feet, "Then turning toward the woman, he said to Simon, "Do you see this woman? I entered your house; you gave me no water for my feet, but she has bathed my feet with her tears and dried them with her hair" (Luke 7:44). On another occasion, he dined with Levi, the tax collector, after calling Levi to follow him. Afterward, "Then Levi gave a great banquet for him in his house; and there was a large crowd of tax collectors and others sitting [reclining] at the table with them" (Luke 5:29) along with other high-class people.

At that time, the upper class reclined on sofas during their meals and had their feet washed by servants. Jesus' statements and behaviors seem to indicate a person who was accustomed to this kind of luxury. His opposition to washing his hands came from this background because the upper echelons of society did not need to wash their hands before eating, because they did not engage in manual labor. They would have had their feet washed.

Many people around Jesus regarded him as a fraud. "And there was considerable complaining about him among the crowds. While some were saying, "He is a good man," others were saying, "No, he is deceiving the crowd" (John 7:12; c.f. John 6:66). His teaching often provoked extreme reactions, "When they heard this, all in the synagogue were filled with rage. They got up, drove him out of the town, and led him to the brow of the hill on which their town was built, so that they might hurl him off the cliff" (Luke 4:28–29).

Jesus' disciples and later *minim* (Judeo-Christians) were associated with the "close to the government" crowd. They were portrayed as publicans (tax collectors) or those with family ties to such circles. The "philosopher" in Shabbat 116a-b refers to a Christian magistrate who was in charge of collecting taxes in the land of Israel. Additionally, it seems the Judeo-Christians were also in charge of collecting taxes in Babylonia (Avodah Zarah 4a, 65a).

This analysis reveals something about Jesus or the early Judeo-Christians. Given that the Gospels are mostly not historical documents and meant to give a historical context to Paul's gospel, I think it is more likely that they reveal traits about Jesus' later followers in the first century CE. However, it is not impossible to see some traces of memories related to the historical Jesus the Nazarene, who would have been a man of some wealth, given his status in Jewish society.

Does the Talmud reveal anything about Jesus' lifestyle beyond what we have seen so far?

The Talmud records that Jesus was a practitioner of magic and had his body tattooed (a violation of Jewish law in Makkot 3:6). However, the Talmud also indicates that he was a "fool", an unfortunate translation of the *halakhic* category of "*shoteh*" (denoting mental illness, "insane" in earlier sources).

> *Shabbat 104b*
> If **one** unwittingly **scratches** letters **on his flesh** on Shabbat, Rabbi Eliezer deems him liable to bring a sin-offering and the Sages deem him exempt. **It was taught** in a *baraita* that **Rabbi Eliezer said to the Rabbis: Didn't** the infamous **ben Stada take** magic **spells out of Egypt in a scratch on his flesh? They said to him: He was a fool, and you cannot cite proof from a fool.**

The Rabbis were sensitive to mental illness in matters of *halakhah*. The definition of *shoteh* is found in Ḥagigah 3b (and 4a). They recognized a scale from one who is "completely insane" (i.e. schizophrenic, etc.), one who "goes in and out of insanity" (manic depressive, bipolar, etc.) and one who is "insane in only one domain" (i.e. delusional disorder). The parameters of this continuum are found in several places in Rabbinic literature.[7] The Rabbis deemed the *shoteh* as lacking critical judgment to perform *mitzvot* and, therefore, a *shoteh* is exempt from mitzvot (Ḥagigah 2b). Most importantly for our discussion, the *shoteh* is exempt from certain forms of punishment (Ḥagigah 3b).

---

7. *Ketubbot* 20a; *Yevamot* 113b; *Nedarim* 36a; *Gittin* 5a, 23a; *Rosh ha-Shana* 28a; Palestinian Talmud, *Ketubbot* 1:25b; Palestinian Talmud, *Gittin* 2:44a)

The Gospels present several moments when Jesus is thought to be insane. Most notably, his family thought so, and the scribes thought he was demon-possessed (Mark 3:21–22). Many crowds thought he was insane or demon-possessed too.[8] Obviously Jesus denied having a demon (John 8:48–49), but the public was not convinced.[9] The Greek word used for "madman" is *exeste*, meaning *shoteh*.

It seems the Pharisees in the Gospels perceived that Jesus might have been a *shoteh* and sought to warn him of potential danger to his life. Luke preserves this memory in his Gospel, even saying, "At that very hour some Pharisees came and said to him, "Get away from here, for Herod wants to kill you" (Luke 13:31).

Of course, it is impossible to diagnose someone from over two thousand years ago. However, it is important to note that this was a memory preserved by *both* the Gospels and the Talmud, making it *more* likely to be true or, if not true, at least a common perception, true. It certainly changes one's perception of Jesus and his ultimate ending, making the story that much more tragic.[10]

8. John 7:20; John 10:19–20

9. John 8:52; Mark 3:11–12

10. Mental illness was also associated with the messianic claimants from the first century CE, see: Lenowitz, Harris. *Jewish Messiah*

What Did Jesus Teach?

THERE IS CONSIDERABLY LESS material in the Talmud concerning the teaching of Jesus, which is also the case with our earliest Christian sources (Paul). The latter does not mention Jesus' teaching much at all, except for a few cases of direct revelation, i.e. things that the spiritual Christ revealed *only* to Paul. These are not of value to understand the nature of what Jesus himself taught.

There are some references to Jesus' teaching in the Talmud: in one case, we have an independent teaching not attested in the Gospels[1] and in another we have a reference to a famous passage in the Gospel of Matthew. We can also do a bit of guesswork to find out what else Jesus *might* have taught, particularly on matters that would have gotten him in trouble with the establishment of the time.

Before examining Jesus' teachings, it is important to note something about Jesus' *movements* in the Gospels. The Rabbis do not preserve much about where Jesus went in his life, other than his association with Lod, but the Gospels do. First, the centers of Rabbinic learning *after* the destruction of the Temple were in Caesarea Maritima, Sepphoris, and Tiberias. Now, it is unknown whether these were centers of *Pharisaic* learning in the time of Jesus, but we might make an assumption that they had been. It is interesting to note that Jesus never enters these cities explicitly in the Gospels. Jesus is known to have gone to Bethsaida[2] on the eastern side of the Sea of Galilee,

---

1. Called an *agraphon* in Jesus studies, potentially authentic sayings of Jesus not found in the canonical Gospels. See, Ehrman, Bart and Zlatko Plese. *The Other Gospels.*

2. Mark 8:22–26

Cana[3], east of Sepphoris, Capernaum on many occasions, which is north of Tiberias, in the nearby village of Chorazin[4], Gennesaret[5], Nain[6] further south, Nazareth of course, and other various locations around the Sea of Galilee. Jesus also leaves the Galilee to go east to the Decapolis and Perea, and south to Samaria, and Jerusalem and Judea. The city of Lod (Lydda), associated with Jesus in the Talmud, is far away from any of the Gospel locations, except Emmaus, which is mentioned as a post-Resurrection story in Luke.[7]

Jesus certainly interacts with Pharisees, Scribes, and Sadducees throughout the Gospels. Using the Gospel of Matthew as a basis, Jesus first encounters a scribe who comes to follow him after the Sermon on the Mount (Matthew 8:18–22), but Jesus seemingly rejects his offer, retorting with his saying that "Foxes have holes, and birds of the air have nests; but the Son of Man has nowhere to lay his head" (v. 20). Jesus leaves to cross the Sea of Galilee before returning to his "own town", presumably Capernaum. Here, Jesus encounters a group of scribes, who witness his healing of a paralytic and forgiving his sins (Matthew 9:2–8). Afterward, Jesus finds Matthew the Tax Collector, who joins his movement. When Jesus dines with Matthew and his friends, the Pharisees inquire about Jesus' choice of dining with this crowd (Matthew 9:9–13), but a synagogue leader subsequently comes to Jesus to ask him to heal his daughter (Matthew 9:18–26). After this episode, Jesus interacts with the Pharisees on the Sabbath, when his disciples pluck grains to eat (Matthew 12:1–8); Jesus then heals a man in the synagogue (9:9–14). The Pharisees and scribes are found throughout Galilee as Jesus interacts with them in each episode. They also come from Jerusalem (15:1–9) to question Jesus on matters of Jewish law and custom.

It seems that the Pharisees mostly are *looking* for Jesus in the Gospel of Matthew, as the Gospel uses phrases like "when they saw this" "when they came to Jesus" etc. Jesus does not seek them out or go to their centers. He rarely goes to Jerusalem or Judea, nor does he enter the centers of population in the Galilee, Sepphoris or Tiberias. If Jesus were ostracized by the Pharisees, it would make perfect sense for him to wish to avoid them at all costs.

3. John 2:1–11
4. Matthew 11:23; Luke 10:13–15
5. Matthew 14:34–36; Mark 6:53–56
6. Luke 7:11–17
7. Additionally, Peter travels to Lod in the book of Acts (9:32–38).

For one of the references to Jesus' teaching, we return to Rabbi Eliezer ben Hyrcanus, who was excommunicated from the rabbinic circle. We saw him earlier in conjunction with our discussion on what Jesus' name was. He was healed by a Christian and taught some words of heresy. In the Tosefta version of this story those words are not revealed, but in the Babylonian Talmud, we do have a record of Jesus' teaching.

As always, we must understand this *sugya* (piece of Talmud) in its context. The *mishnah* that it is elaborating on deals with what items may be sold to gentiles. The subject of the entire tractate is idol worship and each *mishnah* details a particular case vis-a-vis idol worship. Here, the concern is building with gentiles, i.e. establishing business relationships. The concern with building is that one might facilitate the building of sanctuaries for idol worship. Later, the Gemara presents cases where Rabbis were involved with local legal authorities, and this brings us back to Rabbi Eliezer.

Rabbi Eliezer[8] is arrested for heresy and, due to a miscommunication, is exempted from the charges and its penalties. Eliezer was distraught over this charge and considered it a great sin. One of his students continues to try to console him and he relates the story of what heresy was pleasing to him that caused this arrest. The story takes place in Sepphoris, near Jesus' hometown in the Gospels, and relates to a famous Christian in the Talmud, Jacob of Kfar Sekhanya, who taught him one of Jesus the Nazarene's teachings. The subject of the teaching is the *halakhic* (legal) interpretation of the verse, "You shall not bring the payment to a prostitute, or the price of a dog, into the house of the Lord your God" (Deuteronomy 23:19). The legal question is this, "What is the *halakha*: Is it permitted to make from the payment to a prostitute for services rendered a bathroom for a High Priest in the Temple?" This was Jesus' teaching about how to interpret the verse, "He said to me: Jesus the Nazarene taught me the following: It is permitted, as derived from the verse: "For of the payment to a prostitute she has gathered them, and to the payment to a prostitute they shall return" (Micah 1:7). Since the coins came from a place of filth, let them go to a place of filth and be used to build a bathroom." Rabbi Eliezer erred by not distancing himself from heresy and the authorities, citing a verse to support this prohibition, "Remove your way far from her, and do not come near the entrance of her house" (Proverbs 5:8). After that, there is an alternative reading of the

---

8. Schäfer Peter. *Jesus in the Talmud* p. 43 quotes Maier in an alternative translation of the Tosefta version of this story which suggests that Eliezer joined a forbidden meal (*symposium*) perhaps a Christian *agape* or orgiastic cult (*Bacchanalia*).

passage given to discuss prostitution and finally a rabbinic response to Jesus' teaching, which results in a different reading of the passage.

Here is the story in full:

Avodah Zarah 16a–17a[9]

MISHNA: One may not sell bears, or lions, or any item that can cause injury to the public, to gentiles. One may not build with them a basilica [*basileki*], a tribunal [gardom], a stadium [*itztadeyya*], or a platform. But one may build with them small platforms [*bimmusiot*] and bathhouses. Even in this case, once he reaches the arched chamber in the bath where the gentiles put up objects of idol worship, it is prohibited to build it. . . .

GEMARA: The Sages taught: When Rabbi Eliezer was arrested and charged with heresy by the authorities, they brought him up to a tribunal to be judged. A certain judicial officer [*hegemon*] said to him: Why should an elder like you engage in these frivolous matters of heresy?

Rabbi Eliezer said to him: The Judge is trusted by me to rule correctly. That officer thought that Rabbi Eliezer was speaking about him; but in fact he said this only in reference to his Father in Heaven. Rabbi Eliezer meant that he accepted God's judgment, i.e., if he was charged he must have sinned to God in some manner. The officer said to him: Since you put your trust in me, you are acquitted [*dimos*]; you are exempt.

When Rabbi Eliezer came home, his students entered to console him for being accused of heresy, which he took as a sign of sin, and he did not accept their words of consolation. Rabbi

9. The version of this story in Qohelet Rabba, a midrashic collection, is slightly more organized[Jacob:]

"It is written in your Torah: You shall not bring the hire of a harlot or the pay of a dog22 into the house of the Lord, your God [in payment] for any vow [for both of these are abhorrent to the Lord, your God] (Deut. 23:19). What is to be done with them (the money)?"I [R. Eliezer] told him: "They are prohibited [for every use]."

He [Jacob] said to me: "They are prohibited as an offering, but it is permissible to dispose of them."

I answered: "In that case, what is to be done with them.

He said to me: "Let bath-houses and privies be made with them." I answered: "You have well spoken because [this particular] Halakha escaped my memory for the moment."

When he saw that I acknowledged his words, he said to me: "Thus said So-and-so (*ploni*): From filth they came and to filth shall they go out (= on filth they should be expended), as it is said: For from the hire of a harlot was it gathered, and to the hire of a harlot shall it re- turn (Mic. 1:7)—Let them be spent on privies for the public!"

This [interpretation] pleased me, and on that account I was ar- rested for heresy (*minut*). (quoted from Schäfer, *Jesus in the Talmud*, p. 43).

Akiva said to him: My teacher, allow me to say one matter from all of that which you taught me. Rabbi Eliezer said to him: Speak. Rabbi Akiva said to him: My teacher, perhaps some statement of heresy came before you and you derived pleasure from it, and because of this you were held responsible by Heaven. Rabbi Eliezer said to him: Akiva, you are right, as you have reminded me that once I was walking in the upper marketplace of Tzippori, and I found a man who was one of the students of Jesus the Nazarene, and his name was Ya'akov of Kefar Sekhanya. He said to me: It is written in your Torah: "You shall not bring the payment to a prostitute, or the price of a dog, into the house of the Lord your God" (Deuteronomy 23:19). What is the *halakha*: Is it permitted to make from the payment to a prostitute for services rendered a bathroom for a High Priest in the Temple? And I said nothing to him in response.

He said to me: Jesus the Nazarene taught me the following: It is permitted, as derived from the verse: "For of the payment to a prostitute she has gathered them, and to the payment to a prostitute they shall return" (Micah 1:7). Since the coins came from a place of filth, let them go to a place of filth and be used to build a bathroom.

And I derived pleasure from the statement, and due to this, I was arrested for heresy by the authorities, because I transgressed that which is written in the Torah: "Remove your way far from her, and do not come near the entrance of her house" (Proverbs 5:8). "Remove your way far from her," this is a reference to heresy; "and do not come near the entrance of her house," this is a reference to the ruling authority. The Gemara notes: And there are those who say a different interpretation: "Remove your way far from her," this is a reference to heresy and the ruling authority; "and do not come near the entrance of her house," this is a reference to a prostitute. And how much distance must one maintain from a prostitute? Rav Ḥisda said: Four cubits.

With regard to the derivation of the verse by Jesus the Nazarene, the Gemara asks: And what do the Sages derive from this phrase: "Payment to a prostitute"? The Gemara answers: They explain it in accordance with the opinion of Rav Ḥisda, as Rav Ḥisda says: Any prostitute who hires herself out to others for money will become so attached to this practice that ultimately, when others no longer wish to hire her, she will hire others to engage in intercourse with her. As it is stated: "And in that you gave payment, and no payment is given to you, therefore you are contrary" (Ezekiel 16:34).

93

Jesus read the passage in Deuteronomy 23:19 and saw a connection of using the funds from prostitution to fund filthy things. The Rabbis read the text more as a condemnation of the work of prostitution. This text presents a common type of *halakhic* disagreement between one Rabbi who offers a lenient interpretation of a law and another who offers a more stringent interpretation. In this case, Rabbi Eliezer offers the more stringent interpretation but finds the lenient opinion in the name of Jesus to be more appealing. In most cases, the lenient opinion becomes the settled law, *halakhah*, yet, in this case, because it is a *min* (heretic) who offers the lenient approach, the Rabbis reject this opinion.[10]

This teaching reminds me of the story in the Gospels where the Pharisees ask Jesus about taxation to Rome and he responds by asking to see a coin. He asks whose face is on the coin and responds by saying, "Give to the emperor the things that are the emperor's, and to God the things that are God's." This type of thinking resonates between the two passages. It seems almost as a type of classification and makes sense if considered from a Gnostic point of view, which would have held suspicion for the physical world, especially in the Temple. Does this short teaching reveal something about Jesus' feelings about the Temple in Jerusalem? Amazingly, he seems willing to "fund" aspects of its upkeep (here of the High Priest) with unorthodox funding. We will come back to that in a moment, but first, we need to examine the other record of Jesus' teaching in the Talmud.

This occurs in another incident also tangentially involving Rabbi Eliezer, within a discussion about sacred texts and which texts can be saved from a fire. The *sugya* starts with a pun from Rabbi Meir talking about Christian texts, the *Evangelion*, as the Rabbis seem to know it. Using Hebrew words, Rabbi Meir describes it as a "wicked folio" and Rabbi Yohanan as a "sinful folio." Then enters Imma Shalom, the wife of Rabbi Eliezer ben Hyrcanus and the sister of Rabban Gamliel. These are not ordinary people, but important, high-ranking people in rabbinic circles.

Imma Shalom knows of a "philosopher" in her neighborhood. This must be some kind of judge or official because he believes himself to be of good repute and does not accept bribes. Imma Shalom and her brother and husband want to mock this Christian (it is assumed in the text that he

---

10. Schäfer *Jesus in the Talmud*, p. 44. Schäfer also reads this text as Rabbi Eliezer admitting to guilt in matters of prostitution and heresy, proposing that Eliezer had participated in ritualistic sexual orgies. He relates this to a rabbinic response against Christianity, particularly given Jesus' own association with sexual impropriety in his parentage.

is). They engage in a series of tests to trick the philosopher and engage in a battle of words with him. We then have two teachings from the *avon gilyon*.

First, Imma Shalom sends her brother before him with a golden lamp asking for judgment. Imma Shalom says she wants a share in her father's estate. The judge says to divide it between the brother and sister. Rabban Gamliel retorts that the Torah says that if there is a son, a daughter does not inherit. The philosopher responds with a condemnation, "Since the day you were exiled from your land, the Torah of Moses was taken away and the *avon gilyon* was given in its place. It is written in the *avon gilyon*: A son and a daughter shall inherit alike." We will return to understand what these teachings mean later, but first, the second teaching.

They returned the next day and brought a donkey and asked for a judgment. Rabban Gamliel had read the *avon gilayon* and cites, "I did not come to subtract from the Torah of Moses, and I did not come to add to the Torah of Moses." Although the wording is different, this is a clear reference to a passage in the Gospel of Matthew, "Do not think that I have come to abolish the law or the prophets; I have come not to abolish but to fulfill" (Matthew 5:17). Gamliel quotes this passage to refute what the philosopher had said earlier about inheritance and daughters. This passage reveals that the Torah still stood as the legal standard and that the daughter could not inherit if there were a son. The end of the passage is a *midrashic* reference:

> *Shabbat 116a-b*
> **Rabbi Meir would call** the Christian writing, the Evangelion, the **wicked folio** [aven gilyon]; **Rabbi Yoḥanan** called it the **sinful folio** [avon gilyon].
> The Gemara relates: **Imma Shalom, the wife of Rabbi Eliezer, was Rabban Gamliel's sister. There was** a Christian **philosopher** [pilosofa] **in their neighborhood who disseminated** about himself **the reputation that he does not accept bribes. They wanted to mock him** and reveal his true nature. **She** privately **gave him a golden lamp, and** she and her brother **came before him,** approaching him as if they were seeking judgment. **She said to** the philosopher: **I want to share** in the inheritance **of my father's estate. He said to them: Divide** it. Rabban Gamliel **said to him: It is written in our** Torah: **In a situation** where there is a **son, the daughter does not inherit.** The philosopher **said to him: Since the day you were exiled from your land, the Torah of Moses was taken away and the** avon gilyon **was given** in its place. **It is written in** the *avon gilyon*: **A son and a daughter shall inherit alike.**

The next day Rabban Gamliel **brought** the philosopher **a Libyan donkey.** Afterward, Rabban Gamliel and his sister came before the philosopher for a judgment. **He said to them: I proceeded to the end** of the avon gilayon, **and it is written: I,** *avon gilayon,* **did not come to subtract from the Torah of Moses, and I did not come to add to the Torah of Moses. And it is written there: In a situation** where there is a **son, the daughter does not inherit. She said to him: May your light shine like a lamp,** alluding to the lamp she had given him. **Rabban Gamliel said to him: The donkey came and kicked the lamp,** thereby revealing the entire episode.

Now, let us compare the three teachings, first reconsidering Jesus' *halakhic* teaching in Avodah Zarah 16a-17a. In the Gospels, there is little that can be considered legal, *halakhic* teaching, especially in any style resembling the proto-Rabbis. Some have argued that Jesus' teaching on divorce is a type of *halakhic* teaching;[11] however, although it does resemble *halakhic* teaching, it is more likely a judaization of Paul's teaching on divorce, which amounts to a complete prohibition. It is interesting that Matthew tries to work that teaching back into a Jewish context by providing some conditions around which divorce might be possible. This is a re-working of Paul's teaching into a proto-rabbinic framework, relying on the debate between the Schools of Hillel and Shammai to make "Jesus of Nazareth's" teaching more overtly Jewish.

Assuming we cannot really know whether or not this is authentic, let us consider that it is. First, it shows that the Rabbis had access to some independent, alternative traditions about Jesus not even preserved among Church historians.[12] There is nothing like this recorded in Epiphanius or Eusebius where they record some instances of divergence between the Jewish Gospels and the canonical Gospels. Here, Jesus speaks like a rabbi. He uses the rhetorical style found throughout the Talmud. He is presented by Rabbi Eliezer as offering a *halakhic* proof for his legal position, and relies on the same methods that other Rabbis would. If Jesus was a student of Rabbi Yehoshua ben Peraḥyah, then he would have had a rabbinic education and taught their rhetorical style. It is not too far-fetched to believe that he developed some *halakhic* positions of his own before he was excommunicated.

---

11. This was argued by Sigal, *The Halakhah of Jesus.*

12. This was argued by Howard, *Hebrew Gospel.*

[With regard to] "You shall not bring the payment to a prostitute, or the price of a dog, into the house of the Lord your God" (Deuteronomy 23:19). What is the *halakha*: Is it permitted to make from the payment to a prostitute for services rendered a bathroom for a High Priest in the Temple? Jesus the Nazarene taught me the following: It is permitted, as derived from the verse: "For of the payment to a prostitute she has gathered them, and to the payment to a prostitute they shall return" (Micah 1:7)

The next element of teaching is interesting because I believe it confirms a suspicion about Jesus and the early movement itself. First, we have more of a theological statement from the philosopher, which is not stated as coming from the *avon gilyon*. It states that the Torah has been taken away and the *avon gilyon* given "since the day you were exiled from your land." This is a fascinating statement, since the Jews had been exiled for some time when this statement would have been made, presumably in the second century CE. Is this a form of the belief held by the Nasaraeans (before Jesus), Nazoraeans and Ebionites, that the Torah was corrupted? It seems to me that this is what is being said, i.e. *because the Torah was 'taken away' or corrupt, the avon gilyon was given [to correct it].* The following statement about the rules of inheritance shows a place where the Nazarenes 'corrected' Torah.

Since the day you were exiled from your land, the Torah of Moses was taken away and the *avon gilyon* was given in its place. It is written in the *avon gilyon*: A son and a daughter shall inherit alike.

The final teaching seems to contradict the statement of the philosopher. If Jesus said he came not to subtract or add to the Torah, how could the *avon gilyon* contradict the teaching of Torah? If what we presented above is true, then it was probably defended by saying that Jesus did not want to add or subtract from the *uncorrupted* Torah, but the text they had at that time was not the correct Torah. In its context in the Gospel of Matthew, this statement in 5:17 begins the so-called "Antitheses" where Jesus is presented as changing some aspects of Torah teaching. I always read those passages as Jesus building fences around the Torah, in the rabbinic fashion, but now I see it more as an example of Jesus presenting the true Torah to his new covenant community.

I did not come to subtract from the Torah of Moses, and I did not come to add to the Torah of Moses.

Did the Rabbis have access to the Gospels? I think so. There are references in Epiphanius to records kept in the *geniza* in Tiberias, where several Gospels were stored, as well as the book of Acts. Did they also have access to *different* Gospels not preserved by the Church? That is harder to answer but, after looking at these texts, I believe they did.

Did Jesus Perform Miracles?

THE TALMUD DOES NOT preserve any memories of Jesus performing miracles, but includes a number of stories of *Christians* performing miracles during the tannaitic period (second century CE). It is unclear whether Jesus himself was a miracle-worker.

Jesus is strongly associated with magic in the Talmud, and, if he did use magic to perform healing, perhaps the Gospels include some memory of how he used magic. There are a number of instances of Jesus using magical techniques to cause healing, most notably the use of saliva in healing. In one story, Jesus puts his fingers into a deaf man's ears, spits, and touches his tongue (Mark 7:31–35). In another instance, Jesus puts saliva on a blind man's eyes to heal him, but warns him not to go back to his village (Mark 8:22–25). The Gospel of Mark also preserves Aramaic words of Jesus spoken over cured individuals, such as "*Talitha koum* (little girl, rise)" (Mark 5:41) and "*Ephphatha* (be opened)" (Mark 7:34).

The Talmud includes various magical remedies for various ailments, most notably prescribing a variety of incantations for different situations; magic itself was even permissible if it was for healing.[1] Spiritual entities, the names of God and righteous saints were added to give one's incantation more efficacy.[2] Amulets and talismans also played an important role in magical healing, as well as serving a preventative role in avoiding such ailments (Shabbat 67a). Sometimes specific words or formulas were designated for a specific illness (Pesaḥim 112b).

1. Shabbat 66b-67a, Gittin 67b
2. Shabbat 67b, Sanhedrin 101a

However, there were limits to magic. In Sanhedrin 90a, "one who whispers over a wound and says [an invocation for healing]" has no place in the World-to-Come [afterlife].[3] The Gemara expands on this statement and shows what is permitted and prohibited. The use of saliva for healing was prohibited, "[The case] where one spits [because] one does not mention the name of Heaven over spittle" (Sanhedrin 101a). This was seen as a profanation of holy things, including God's name, but Scripture more broadly, as these were used as invocations in healing.

If this is the case, then Jesus' use of saliva would indicate he was using prohibited magic from the Rabbinic perspective, which would merit his excommunication and later execution, given the severity of the prohibition in Sanhedrin 90a. Additionally, the preservation of possible invocations whispered over healed individuals would place Jesus in violation of the Mishnah in Sanhedrin 10:1 (Babylonian Talmud Sanhedrin 90a).

Still, there is no *direct* reference in the Talmud to Jesus healing or using magic. All of our earliest references to Jesus lack any sort of miracle tradition, most importantly in the Epistles of Paul. This is to be expected, given our previous discussion of the type of figure Jesus Christ is in Paul's theology. The focus of Paul's groups was not the historical man, Jesus, but the spiritual Christ. Still, there are some links to the historical life of Jesus in Paul (which will be examined in depth later), even if they are mere kernels. There is no indication that Jesus had a healing or any other ministry: the focus of Jesus' work in Paul is his death and resurrection. The few instances of Jesus' influence beyond that are direct revelations that Paul received, such as the tradition of the Lord's Supper.

The Talmud has several stories of *Christians* performing miracles during the tannaitic period (second century CE). Could it be possible that Jesus himself never performed a miracle? Is it more likely that his followers began to perform them *in his name*?

I think either possibility is likely. However, if he did not perform miracles, then why was the tradition so closely associated with him later? It is entirely likely that Jesus' followers began to perform magical healings in Israel after his death, using the magical incantation bowls. These types of healings were performed "in the name of" a famous person or rabbi. The various stories of *Christians* in the Talmud indicate this was taking place.

---

3. The earlier Tosefta and Jerusalem Talmud do not share this strict prohibition, as do other parts of the Babylonian Talmud (Tosefta Shabbat 7:23, Jerusalem Talmud Shabbat 14:3–5).

Paul's groups must have had some knowledge of the healing ministries of the Christians in the Holy Land, as various Christian groups became aware of and communicated with each other.

Mark, or whoever wrote the Gospel in his name, began the work of telling the 'origin' of Paul's gospel. The structure he created became the framework which subsequent authors used. Even when Matthew and Luke disagree with Mark, and they often do, they maintain his structure in the Gospel story. The bulk of Mark's Gospel is a collection of stories of how Jesus healed throughout Galilee during his life.

I believe this is a reading back into history the stories of miraculous healings Mark had heard about from the Galilean Christians. It becomes a logical presupposition: if all of these Christians can perform miracles in the Lord's name, then all the more so should Jesus have been a master miracle-worker himself.

If he *did* perform miracles, why are there no stories or references to this in the rabbinic tradition? It is a question that, unfortunately, we cannot answer.

Who Were Jesus' Disciples?

B OTH THE RABBINIC AND CHRISTIAN traditions portray Jesus as having been a teacher with disciples of his own, in addition to being a student of another teacher. Of course that teacher is different, depending on the narrative, and the type of teacher also differs, depending on who his teacher was reported to have been. Jesus must have been a teacher of some renown, if he attracted a following of any substantial size, but it should be noted that the climate was ripe for cultivating movements throughout the Hasmonean and Roman period in Palestine, as we see countless examples of movements forming and disappearing throughout this period.

It is important to remember that the period was one of immense transformation in the political realm and for the Jewish nation. The nation had lost its autonomy and independence under the Hasmoneans, who were certainly a corrupt ruling class, but who provided the Jewish people a sense of national identity as a separate state. It became a vassal state to the Roman Empire and lost any sense of a unique national identity, even if it did maintain its traditional centers in the Temple and Sanhedrin. These institutions had changed over the years and likely never resembled the rabbinic descriptions of them in the Talmud.

This environment sparked a quest for meaning among the Jewish people, as we can see in the proliferation of movements, sects, and military campaigns against the Romans. It seems there was an endless supply of possible responses and solutions to the ills of the Jewish People. We can imagine that the disciples of Jesus fit into this group. They must have found something about his Gnostic teachings to provoke interest for them. Gnosticism has an alternative take on the suffering in the world and attracted a great number of people in the ancient world, due to its understanding of the true nature of the physical world.

In any case, it is impossible to know *who* these people were originally. None of the traditions around their names match, even in Christian records. It is unlikely that any tradition of naming these men would have been maintained in the early years as there would have been no reason to record their names for posterity. We can imagine them passing on Jesus' gnosis after his death for a few generations before a distinct movement began to crystalize. It is also possible that the preserved traditions record different eras of the Jesus movement, as it fractured among the Nasaraeans, Ebionites, Nazarenes, Paulines, Marcionites and other Gnostic groups. I believe the Talmud maintains an earlier memory of Jesus' disciples where there was no apocalyptic community with twelve representatives of the tribes of Israel, later found in the Christian texts. In this case, James, Peter, and John were the "pillars" of the community in Jerusalem before Paul received his visions and, in their generation, the movement began to see splintering, as enough time had passed for different versions of Jesus' story to be passed around.

The Talmud's account of Jesus' followers occurs directly after the account of Jesus' execution, listing the names of five disciples. We will analyze the names of the disciples shortly. However, it must be noted that there are other Rabbis in the Talmud that have five disciples. Was this a rabbinic tradition for scholars, or a coincidence?

One of the more prominent individuals with five disciples was Yohanan ben Zakkai, one of the most important Rabbis of the first century CE. More than any other Rabbi, Yohanan is most responsible for the survival of Pharisaic Judaism after the Destruction of the Second Temple, and the Jewish Encyclopedia describes his importance for the rabbinic movement:

Jewish Encyclopedia
The most important tanna in the last decade of the Second Temple, and, after the destruction of Jerusalem, the founder and first president of the academy at Jabneh. According to the theory formulated in the Mishnah (Pirke Avot 2:8), that traditions were handed down through an unbroken chain of scholars, Johanan, in receiving the teachings of Hillel and Shammai, formed the last link in that chain. But it is rather as a pupil of Hillel than of Shammai that he is known (Sukkot 28a). Before his death Hillel is said to have prophetically designated Johanan, his youngest pupil, as "the father of wisdom" and "the father of coming generations"

(Jerusalem Nedarim 39b). Like that of Hillel, Johanan's life was divided into periods of forty years each. In the first of these he followed a mercantile pursuit; in the second he studied; and in the third he taught (Rosh Hashanah 30b). Another version has it (*Sifre*, Deut. 35:7) that in the last forty years of his life he was a leader of Israel. If the last statement be accepted as approximately correct, and it is assumed that Johanan lived at the latest one decade after the destruction of Jerusalem, his public activity as the recognized leader of the pharisaic scribes must have begun between the years 30 and 40 of the common era.

Rabbi Yoḥanan's disciples are described in the Mishnah. He taught other important Rabbis who contributed to the development of rabbinic tradition in the Mishnah, including Rabbi Eliezer ben Hyrcanus, a figure who has shown up in multiple instances in our story about the life of Jesus the Nazarene.

Pirke Avot 2:8
> Rabban Yohanan ben Zakkai had five disciples and they were these: Rabbi Eliezer ben Hyrcanus, Rabbi Joshua ben Hananiah, Rabbi Yose, the priest, Rabbi Shimon ben Nethaneel and Rabbi Eleazar ben Araḥ.

Another Rabbi of the generation after Rabbi Yoḥanan, Rabbi Yehuda ben Bava, also had five disciples. He was involved in a crisis about whether a single rabbi could ordain another.

Jewish Encyclopedia
> Tanna of the second century; martyred (at the age of seventy) during the persecutions under Hadrian. At that time the government forbade, among other things, the ordination of rabbis, an infraction of the law being punished by the death of both ordainer and ordained and by the destruction of the city in which the ordination took place. Judah b. Baba nevertheless called together five—according to others, seven—disciples qualified for ordination, took them to a defile between Usha and Shefaram, and duly ordained them. They were detected, and while his disciples, at his urging, fled, he, too old and feeble to flee, was slain by the Roman soldiery, who hurled 300 javelins at his body (Sanhedrin 14a). So great was the fear of the Romans that people did not dare even to praise him publicly.

Yehuda ben Bava ordained Rabbis Meir, Yehuda, Shimon, Yossei and Elazar ben Shammua, all of which played some role in the development of Judaism after the fall of the Temple.

> *Sanhedrin 14b*
> What did Rabbi Yehuda ben Bava do? He went and sat be-
> tween two large mountains, between two large cities, and between
> two Shabbat boundaries: Between Usha and Shefaram, and there
> he ordained five elders. And they were: Rabbi Meir, and Rabbi Ye-
> huda, and Rabbi Shimon, and Rabbi Yosei, and Rabbi Elazar ben
> Shammua. Rav Avya adds that Rabbi Neḥemya was also among
> those ordained. This incident indicates that ordination can be per-
> formed by a single Sage.

Do these parallels have any impact on our thinking about Jesus the Nazarene? I am not sure that they do, but perhaps I am wrong. It might be an interesting parallel that has no practical consequences, or it could imply something about Jesus and his stature in the rabbinic community.

Let us examine the text in the Talmud, which lists Jesus' disciples under the names: Mattai, Nakai, Netzer, Buni, and Toda. The Gemara begins by citing the *baraita* (formal legal pronouncement) about the disciples of Jesus:

> *Sanhedrin 43a*
> the Sages taught: Jesus the Nazarene had five disciples: Mattai,
> Nakai, Netzer, Buni, and Toda.

The *sugya* then goes through each disciple and a snippet of the trial presented against them by the Sanhedrin. Mattai is the first disciple the Gemara describes.

> **They brought Mattai in** to stand trial. Mattai **said to** the judges:
> **Shall Mattai be executed?** But **isn't it written: "When** [matai]
> **shall I come and appear before God?"** (Psalms 42:3). Mattai
> claimed that this verse alludes to the fact he is righteous. **They said
> to him: Yes, Mattai shall be executed, as it is written: "When**
> [matai] **shall he die, and his name perish?"** (Psalms 41:6).

The nature of each trial is representative of rabbinic rhetoric which tries to establish Scriptural links to rabbinic practices. Here they look for linguistic connections between the names of the disciples and references in the Tanakh. It is hard not to mention that *Mattai* sounds like the name of the Apostle Matthew, who supposedly wrote the Gospel in his name (according to tradition). Matthew's name in Greek is *Matthaios,* and *Matityahu* in Hebrew, and shortened to *Mattai* in Aramaic, the vernacular of the day. In Hebrew, the word *matai* means "when" which the Rabbis use to create a connection to the verses in Psalms used to proceed with his trial. It is highly unlikely that these were considered legal records of the actual trials but serve more like midrashic interpretations of the disciples.

The next disciple mentioned is Nakai. Before examining the text about him in the *sugya,* I want to present an interesting theory. G.R.S. Mead believes that Nakai is the same as Nakdimon ben Guryon, because there is a tradition that Nakdimon's true name is *Buni.*

> *Ta'anit 20a*
>
> As the master entered the bathhouse in his joy, Nakdimon entered the Temple in a state of sadness. He wrapped himself in his prayer shawl and stood in prayer.
>
> He said before God: Master of the Universe, it is revealed and known before You that I did not act for my own honor, nor did I act for the honor of my father's house. Rather, I acted for Your honor, so that there should be water for the Festival pilgrims. Immediately the sky became overcast and rain fell until the twelve cisterns were filled with water, and there was even more water, so that they overflowed.
>
> As the master left the bathhouse, Nakdimon ben Guryon left the Temple. When they met one another, Nakdimon said to him: Give me the money you owe me for the extra water you received. The official said to him: I know that the Holy One, Blessed be He, has shaken His world and caused rain to fall only for you. However, I still maintain a claim against you, by which I can legally take my coins from you, as you did not pay me on the agreed date, for the sun had already set, and therefore the rain fell onto my property.
>
> Nakdimon went back and entered the Temple, wrapped himself in his prayer shawl, and stood in prayer. He said before God: Master of the Universe, let it be known that You have beloved ones in Your world. Immediately, the clouds scattered and the sun shined. At that time, the master said to him: If the sun had not broken through the clouds, I would have had a claim against you, by which I could have taken my coins from you. A Sage taught: Nakdimon was not his real name; rather his name was Buni. And why was he called Nakdimon? Because the sun broke through [nikdera] for him.

Whether or not these associations can be made is beside the point. This is an example of rabbinic rhetoric and a rhetorical clash with Christianity. Let us take one example, the case of Nakai. The text he presents to defend himself is Exodus 23:7, the Rabbis respond with Psalms 10:8.

> *Sanhedrin 43a*
> Then **they brought Nakai in** to stand trial. Nakai **said** to the judges: **Shall Nakai be executed?** But **isn't it written: "And the innocent [naki] and righteous you shall not slay"** (Exodus 23:7)? **They said to him: Yes, Nakai shall be executed, as it is written: "In secret places he kills the innocent [naki]"** (Psalms 10:8).

The text comes from the Torah, from *Parashat Mishpatim,* a follow-up to the Ten Commandments, in which the details of Mosaic legislation are expanded upon.

> *Exodus 23:7*
> Keep far from a false charge; do not bring death on those who are innocent and in the right, for I will not acquit the wrongdoer.

Two terms are used in this verse, a *naki* and a *tzaddik.* The former is one who is not a *tzaddik,* but one who "who testifies that he knows of evidence in favor of a person who has been convicted of a certain misdemeanor. In such a case the trial is re-opened" (Commentary Or Ḥaim). The verse and allusion to Rabbinic law in Sanhedrin is meant to exonerate Nakai.

The Rabbis respond with a verse from Psalm 10. The verses before this one are a lament to God, asking him why he allows the wicked to scheme against the righteous and why he is absent in times of trouble.

> *Psalms 10:8*
> He lurks in outlying places;
> from a covert he slays the innocent;
> his eyes spy out the hapless.

Radak, a later medieval commentary, adds, "for usually the wicked does not do his wicked work openly, but he sits in ambushes and secret places so that he may beware of the sons of men so that they may not see him. But he cannot beware of the All-seeing God!" While we cannot know if this is what the Rabbis thought, it seems very likely the reason behind their choice of this verse as a rebuttal.

The rest of the *sugya* reads in a similar fashion:

Then **they brought Netzer in** to stand trial. **He said** to the judges: **Shall Netzer be executed?** But **isn't it written: "And a branch** [netzer] **shall grow out of his roots"** (Isaiah 11:1)? **They said to him: Yes, Netzer shall be executed, as it is written: "But you are cast out of your grave like an abhorred branch** [netzer]" (Isaiah 14:19).

Then **they brought Buni in** to stand trial. Buni **said** to the judges: **Shall Buni be executed?** But **isn't it written: "My first-born son** [beni] **is Israel"** (Exodus 4:22)? **They said to him: Yes, Buni shall be executed, as it is written: "Behold, I shall kill your firstborn son** [binkha]" (Exodus 4:23).

Then **they brought Toda in** to stand trial. Toda **said** to the judges: **Shall Toda be executed?** But **isn't it written: "A psalm of thanksgiving** [toda]" (Psalms 100:1)? **They said to him: Yes, Toda shall be executed, as it is written: "Whoever slaughters a thanks-offering** [toda] **honors Me"** (Psalms 50:23).

The Christian narrative is not clear on the names of Jesus' disciples either. Paul mentions Peter, James, and John, as "pillars" in Galatians 1, but does not mention any other disciples by name. They are probably lost to legend. All the Gospels mention Simon, who has either a surname or nickname of Peter. Most of the Gospels agree on most of the disciples, but there are some discrepancies.

Mark	Matthew	Luke
Simon (Peter)	Simon	Simon
James, son of Zebedee	Andrew, brother of	Andrew
John, brother of James	Simon	James (son of Zebedee?)
Andrew	James, son of Zebedee	John
Philip	John, son of Zebedee	Philip
Bartholomew (Nathaniel)	Philip	Bartholomew
Matthew (Levi)	Bartholomew	Matthew
Thomas	Thomas	Thomas
James, son of Alphaeus	Matthew (Levi)	James, son of Alphaeus
Thaddeus	James, son of Alphaeus	Judas, brother of James,
Simon the Canaanite	Lebbaeus	son of Alphaeus
Judas Iscariot	Simon the Canaanite	Judas Iscariot
	Judas Iscariot	

In Mark 2:14, Levi (Matthew) is called the brother of James, son of Al-phaeus, who also has a brother, Judas, in Luke, but Judas is not mentioned in any other Gospel narrative. Mark has Thaddeus, Matthew has Lebbaeus, but mentions his surname is "Thaddeus." John does not include a list of the disciples but mentions by name: Peter, Andrew, the sons of Zebedee, Philip, Nathanael, Thomas, Judas Iscariot, and another Judas.

Was Jesus Betrayed?

JESUS WAS A STUDENT of Yehoshua ben Peraḥyah with Yehudah ben Tabbai and Shimon ben Shataḥ (Sotah 47a). However, not all of Yehoshua's disciples accompanied him to Alexandria. Shimon ben Shetaḥ stayed behind and was hidden by his sister when King Yannai killed the Sages of the day. Yehoshua and Jesus escaped to Egypt, and while it is not clear whether Yehudah ben Tabbai also accompanied them, it is my contention that he did.

> *Sotah 47a*
> The Gemara returns to the incident in which **Yehoshua ben Peraḥya** turned away Jesus the Nazarene: **What is** this incident? **When King Yannai was killing the Sages, Shimon ben Shataḥ was hidden by his sister,** Yannai's wife, while **Rabbi Yehoshua ben Peraḥya went** and **fled to Alexandria of Egypt. When peace was made** between Yannai and the Sages, **Shimon ben Shataḥ sent him** the following letter: **From myself, Jerusalem the holy city, to you, Alexandria of Egypt. My sister, my husband dwells within you, and I am sitting desolate.** Rabbi Yehoshua ben Peraḥya **said:** I can **learn from it that there is peace,** and I can return.

It is when Yehoshua ben Peraḥyah and Jesus returned that they parted ways and all of history would be changed. Yehoshua received the letter from Shimon, saying that it was safe to return. He came back with his disciple Jesus and stayed at an inn along the way. Yehoshua comments on the inn and how beautiful it is, but Jesus understands this to refer to the innkeeper's wife. Yehoshua rebukes Jesus for the impropriety of his statement and ostracizes him, and this is the point when he separated from the Rabbis.

Jesus tried to apologize. This story is remarkable in that it presents Jesus in a semi-positive light, given that he tried to apologize to his teacher several times. The final break between him and Yehoshua occurred due to a misunderstanding, and the latter part of the story is truly heartbreaking. After Jesus left his teacher, thinking he had been rebuked, he turned to idolatry. The exact meaning of this statement is undecipherable: it could refer to some stone idols, but others have more creative readings of the phrase, though in my opinion none of these are convincing. Yehoshua comes to Jesus and begs him to repent, but Jesus cites Yehoshua's own *halakhic* teaching about an inciter: "Whoever sins and causes the masses to sin is not given the opportunity to repent." It is recorded afterward that this is when Jesus turned to idolatry and sorcery, and left the rabbinic circle.

The way the story is read, it seems that the Rabbis are taking some responsibility for this episode, painting Jesus as a repentant sinner. Rabbi Yehoshua's famous teaching, "[G]ive everybody the benefit of the doubt" (Pirke Avot 1:4) becomes much more poignant after having read this story.

Sanhedrin 107b
    What is the incident involving **Yehoshua ben Peraḥya?** The Gemara relates: **When King Yannai was killing the Sages, Yehoshua ben Peraḥya and Jesus, his student, went to Alexandria of Egypt. When there was peace** between King Yannai and the Sages, **Shimon ben Shataḥ sent** a message **to** Yehoshua ben Peraḥya: **From me, Jerusalem, the holy city, to you, Alexandria of Egypt: My sister, my husband is located among you and I sit desolate.** The head of the Sages of Israel is out of the country and Jerusalem requires his return.

    Yehoshua ben Peraḥya understood the message, **arose, came, and happened** to arrive at **a certain inn** on the way to Jerusalem. **They treated him with great honor.** Yehoshua ben Peraḥya **said: How beautiful is this inn.** Jesus, his student, **said to him:** But **my teacher, the eyes of** the innkeeper's wife **are narrow** [terutot]. Yehoshua ben Peraḥya **said to him: Wicked one!** Do **you involve yourself with regard to that** matter, the appearance of a married woman? **He produced four hundred** shofarot **and ostracized him.**

    Jesus **came before** Yehoshua ben Peraḥya **several times** and **said to him: Accept our,** i.e., my, repentance. Yehoshua ben Peraḥya **took no notice of him. One day** Yehoshua ben Peraḥya **was reciting** Shema and Jesus **came before him** with the same request. Yehoshua ben Peraḥya **intended to accept his** request, and **signaled him with his hand** to wait until he completed his prayer.

Jesus did not understand the signal and **thought: He is driving me away. He went** and **stood a brick** upright to serve as an idol **and he bowed to it.** Yehoshua ben Peraḥya then **said to Jesus: Repent.** Jesus **said to him: This** is the tradition that **I received from you: Whoever sins and causes the masses to sin is not given the opportunity to repent. And the Master says: Jesus performed sorcery, incited** Jews to engage in idolatry, **and led Israel astray.** Had Yehoshua ben Peraḥya not caused him to despair of atonement, he would not have taken the path of evil.

The Rabbis even changed their approach to teachers and students after this incident, developing a more lenient style. Rabbi Yehoshua ben Peraḥyah was included in this *baraita* as an example of how *not* to treat a student. The Rabbis do not go so far as to say that Jesus was right in this case, meaning they do not entirely blame Yehoshua but neither do they exonerate him.

> Sotah 47a
> The Sages taught: It should always be the left, weaker, hand that pushes another away and the right, stronger, hand that draws him near. In other words, even when a student is rebuffed, he should be given the opportunity to return. This is not like Elisha, who pushed Gehazi away with both hands, and not like Yehoshua ben Peraḥya, who pushed Jesus the Nazarene, one of his students, away with both hands . . .

Is that the end of the story? I think not. I believe the positivity attributed to Jesus comes from a memory that he might not have committed this awful crime. It might have been someone else who was ostracized by his teacher. We recall that Yehudah ben Tabbai was also a student of Rabbi Yehoshua ben Peraḥyah and "unaccounted" for during the time in Alexandria, meaning there is no record of him in Alexandria, but neither is there any record of him staying in Israel.

In the Jerusalem Talmud, the same story is recounted by Yehudah ben Tabbai, and in this version, Yehudah is in Alexandria with an unnamed student. The people of Jerusalem wrote to have him come back, but this alternative tradition would not put Yehoshua ben Peraḥyah or Jesus in Egypt at all.

> Jerusalem Talmud Ḥagigah 2:2
> From the great Jerusalem to the small Alexandria: How long still will my betrothed live in your midst and I am sitting sorrowful

about him? He took leave and started on a ship. He said, I remember the lady of the house who received us; what is she missing? One of his students told him, her eye is damaged. He told him, you have sinned twice; first that you suspected me, and second that you looked at her. Did I say that she was beautiful in looks? I only said that about her deeds. He was taking offense and he left.

There are few possibilities as to how to approach this problem. There is a stronger impulse to attribute this story to Jesus and Yehoshua, as it occurs in the Babylonian Talmud, yet the evidence of the earlier Jerusalem Talmud should not be ignored.

If Yehudah was the one who left for Egypt and *his* student was the one who was involved in this incident, we have a few possibilities.[1] First, it could be that this is a cryptic reference to Jesus in the Jerusalem Talmud, only associating him as a student of Yehudah ben Tabbai. The Talmud remembers Jesus as a magician, a fact not ignored by scholarship. Why then the confusion?

It must relate to Jesus' practice of magic. Egypt was well-known as a place where magic was practiced, and Jewish magicians were held in high regard in society of the time.[2] Yehudah and Shimon were students of Yehoshua ben Peraḥyah, who later became associated with magic himself, as his name was used in magical incantation bowls. Could it be possible that they thought Jesus had tainted the name of their teacher, associating him with the practice of magic?

Yehudah and Shimon succeeded Yehoshua as the Nasi and *Av Bet Din*, the leaders of the Jewish People at that time (according to Rabbinic

1. There are two alternatives. First, it is *possible* that the attribution of Jesus with Yehoshua ben Peraḥyah could itself be a misattribution, considering these were common, due to the importance of attributing sayings "in the name of" important rabbis (M Avot 6:6; BT Meg 15a; Hul 104b; Nid 19b; Kallah 1:1; Kallah 8:1). Elman (1999 pp. 61–62) notes over 750 cases of alternative attributions in the Talmud, often through misattribution of contemporaries. This could be due to phonetic similarities between the names involved, *Yehoshua; Yehudah; Yeshua* (ישוע, יהודה, יהושע). It is possible that the link between Yehoshua and Yehudah (ben Tabbai) was the original teacher-disciple tradition, which is maintained in Pirke Avot's list of the transmission of the oral tradition (1:8). This fits into the tradition of *zugot* ("pairs") of that part of the chain. Yehoshua ben Perachiah and Nittai the Arbelite pass the tradition to Shimon ben Shetach and Yehudah ben Tabbai. The addition of a third prominent student, Yeshu ben Pantera, distorts the "pairs' tradition and contradicts earlier sources. It's also possible that the Babylonian Rabbis associated Yehoshua ben Perachiah and Jesus through magic, due to the occurrence of both names on magical incantation bowls (Schäfer 2007, p. 38–39.

2. Smith, Morton. *Jesus the Magician*

tradition). They began a campaign against sorcery, going so far as to kill eighty witches in one day. If the tradition was originally anonymous, could Yehudah have begun the process of identifying *Jesus* with the idolatrous student here? Having Jesus be ostracized by his teacher would make him fully outside of the Rabbinic circle and easier to convict; it also paints the Rabbis in a better light by not having a magician among their ranks.

> *Jerusalem Talmud Sanhedrin 6:6*
> Anyone who was stoned is hanged, the words of Rabbi Eliezer. But the Sages say, only the blasphemer and the idolator are hanged. A man is hanged face to the people and a woman face to the pole, the words of Rabbi Eliezer. But the Sages say, a man is hanged
> Rabbi Eliezer said, it happened that Simeon ben Shetaḥ hanged women in Ascalon. They told him, he hanged eighty women, but one does not try two on the same day
> What is Rabbi Eliezer's motive? As the blasphemer, after being stoned must be hanged, so all those condemned to stoning will be hanged. The other sages on the contrary say: the Bible prescribes hanging for the blasphemer alone, because he touches on the essential question of worship (belief in God); also this new penalty is only applicable to criminals of this order (i.e. the idolater in addition to the blasphemer) . . . he made a personal vow that if he were elected president, he would kill all sorcerers . . . Simeon ben Shetaḥ hanged eighty women in Ascalon, but one does not try two on the same day." But the hour needed it.

Shimon ben Shataḥ was fanatical in his opposition to sorcery and would have done anything to remove it. He even lost his own son over the affair with the trial of the witches.

If this reading is true, Jesus was *not* excommunicated by his teacher, but framed by Yehudah ben Tabbai. It is still likely that Jesus was a magician himself, given the other evidence in that regard.

Why Was Jesus Executed?

PERHAPS THE BIGGEST QUESTION vis-a-vis the historical Jesus is the reason for his execution. Was it for blasphemy because he claimed to be Messiah and the Son of God, according to Christian tradition? Was it because he was an apocalyptic messiah who wanted to overthrow the Roman government in Palestine as some scholars have suggested? Who was primarily behind the execution: was it the Jews or the Romans?

In Jewish sources, the death of Jesus is remembered as an *internal Jewish affair*. If we look in the Talmud, in Tractate Sanhedrin, which deals with all manners of trials and court cases in Jewish law, we will find the story of Jesus' execution, as the Rabbis remembered it. First, though, we can establish a bit of chronology using a cryptic reference to Jesus in the Talmud. This passage is cryptic because it does not reference Jesus the Nazarene at all but Balaam, from the Torah, although it is commonly read as a reference to Jesus. It is interpreted as referring to Jesus because a *min* ('heretic') asks the Rabbis about his age when he died. This has been used as evidence to point to a reference to Jesus, because it seems unlikely that a Judeo-Christian would be *that* interested in the character from the Hebrew Scriptures (Jesus and Balaam are also mentioned together in Gittin 56b–57a, establishing a connection between them). The *sugya* tells us that Jesus (here Balaam[1]) was thirty-two or thirty-four years old when he died. This is used to infer Jesus' *possible* age at death, presuming a 100 BCE to 66 BCE lifespan. The latter portion of the *sugya* is used as a possible reference to Pontius Pilate,

---

1. Balaam is presented as an outsider who seduces the people of God to false religion, a traditional picture shared by rabbinic writers, c.f. 2 Pet 2:15, Jude 11; Rev 2:14 (Van Voorst, 2000 p. 110).

being corrupted to Pinehas. I do not see much reason to believe that, but the ending of the text is cryptic and undecipherable.

> *Sanhedrin 106b*
>
> **A certain heretic said to Rabbi Ḥanina: Have you heard how old Balaam was** when he died? Rabbi Ḥanina **said to him: It is not written** explicitly in the Torah. **But from** the fact **that it is written: "Bloody and deceitful men shall not live half their days"** (Psalms 55:24), this indicates that he was **thirty-two or thirty-four years old,** less than half the standard seventy-year lifespan. The heretic **said to him: You have spoken well, I myself saw the notebook of Balaam and it was written therein: Balaam the lame was thirty-two years old when Pinehas the highwayman killed him.**

Returning to Jesus' execution, as presented in the Talmud[2], the *mishnah* discusses a case where if there is reason to acquit the person, then he can be acquitted immediately, but if not he is to be stoned immediately. A crier is supposed to go before and announce what the charge is and who are the witnesses and announce that anyone who knows of a reason to acquit should speak up. The Gemara adds that the transgression must be announced and when it was committed. There is a question about the details of the case and whether the crier should go out before. Then the Gemara presents a *baraita*, an official statement, about Jesus the Nazarene and his execution. This is the charge presented: Jesus the Nazarene is going out to be stoned because he practiced sorcery, incited [people to idol worship],

---

2. Schäfer *Jesus in the Talmud*, quotes Mishnah Sotah 6:4 to summarize the trial process (pp. 66–67): All who are stoned are also hanged (*nitlin*) [afterwards] [on a tree]: (these are) the words of R. Eliezer.

However the Sages said: only the blasphemer (*ha-megaddef*) and the idolater (*ha-<oved avodah zarah*) are hanged.

As to a man, they hang him facing the people, and as to a woman, (they hang her) facing the tree: (these are) the words of R. Eliezer.

However the Sages said: the man is hanged, but the woman is not hanged (at all). [...] How do they hang him?

They drive a post into the ground, and a beam juts from it, and one ties together his two hands one upon the other, and thus does one hang him.

R. Yose says: the post leans against a wall, and one hangs him the way butchers do (it).

And they untie him immediately. Because, if he stays (on the tree) overnight, one transgresses a negative commandment on his account, as it is said: You must not leave his corpse on the tree [overnight], but you must bury him that same day, for he who is hanged (*talui*) is a curse against God (*qilelat elohim*), etc. (Deut. 21:23). That is to say, on what account has this [man] been hanged? Because he cursed the Name, and the Name of Heaven turned out to be profaned.

and led the Jewish people astray. There was no defense for his acquittal and so he was hung on the eve of Passover.

Jesus was a well-known sinner, meaning he did these things *in public*, which implies there were multiple witnesses to speak against him.

> *Sanhedrin 103a*
>
> **Alternatively,** the phrase **"no evil shall befall you"** means **that you will be frightened neither by bad dreams nor by evil thoughts.** "Nor shall any plague come near your tent" means **that you will not have a child or student who overcooks his food in public,** i.e., sins in public and causes others to sin, **such as** in the well-known case of **Jesus the Nazarene.**

The Gemara asks why such a case was possible on his behalf, given the severity of his crimes. This is where we hear that Jesus was "close to the government." Perhaps the non-Jewish authorities had some acquaintance with Jesus and sought to find a reason to acquit him.

> *Sanhedrin 43a*
>
> **MISHNA:** If, after the condemned man is returned to the courthouse, the judges **find** a reason to **acquit him, they** acquit him and **release him** immediately. **But if** they do **not** find a reason to acquit him, **he goes out to be stoned. And a crier goes out before him** and publicly proclaims: **So-and-so, son of so-and-so, is going out to be stoned because he committed such and such a transgression. And so-and-so and so-and-so are his witnesses. Anyone who knows** of a reason to **acquit him should come** forward **and teach** it **on his behalf.**
>
> **GEMARA: Abaye says: And** the crier **must** also publicly **proclaim** that the transgression was committed **on such and such a day, at such and such an hour, and at such and such a place,** as **perhaps there are those who know** that the witnesses could not have been in that place at that time, **and they will come** forward **and render** the witnesses **conspiring witnesses.**
>
> The mishna teaches that **a crier goes out before** the condemned man. This indicates that it is only **before him,** i.e., while he is being led to his execution, that **yes,** the crier goes out, but **from the outset,** before the accused is convicted, he does **not** go out. The Gemara raises a difficulty: **But isn't it taught** in a *baraita*: **On Passover Eve they hung** the corpse of **Jesus the Nazarene** after they killed him by way of stoning. **And a crier went out before him** for **forty days,** publicly proclaiming: **Jesus the Nazarene is going out to be stoned because he practiced sorcery, incited**

people to idol worship, **and led the Jewish people astray. Anyone who knows** of a reason to **acquit him should come** forward **and teach** it **on his behalf. And** the court **did not find** a reason to **acquit him, and** so **they** stoned him and **hung his** corpse **on Passover eve.**

Ulla said: And how can you understand this proof? Was Jesus the Nazarene worthy of conducting a search for a reason to acquit him? He was an inciter to idol worship, and the Merciful One states with regard to an inciter to idol worship: "Neither shall you spare, neither shall you conceal him" (Deuteronomy 13:9). Rather, Jesus was different, as he had close ties with the government, and the gentile authorities were interested in his acquittal. Consequently, the court gave him every opportunity to clear himself, so that it could not be claimed that he was falsely convicted.

Other sources indicate that he was hung (Sanhedrin 46b). Where was he executed? Another part of the Gemara indicates that this occurred in Lydda (Lod) near modern Tel Aviv, *not Jerusalem*, as the Gospels indicate, which was Jesus' hometown.

Babylonian Talmud, Sanhedrin 67a
GEMARA: The mishna teaches: With regard to the case of **an inciter, this is an ordinary person.** The Gemara infers: **The reason** he is executed by stoning is **that he is an ordinary person, but** if he is **a prophet** he is executed **by strangulation,** not by stoning. The mishna states further: **And** it is referring to **one who incites an ordinary person.** The Gemara infers: **The reason** he is executed by stoning is **that** he incited **an individual, but** if he subverted **a multitude** of people, he is executed **by strangulation.**

Consequently, **whose** opinion is expressed in **the mishna? It is** the opinion of **Rabbi Shimon, as it is taught** in a *baraita*: **A prophet who subverted** others to participate in idol worship is executed **by stoning. Rabbi Shimon says:** He is executed **by strangulation. Likewise, the subverters of an idolatrous city** are executed **by stoning. Rabbi Shimon says: By strangulation.**

The Gemara challenges: **Say the last clause** of the mishna, i.e., say the following mishna: With regard to the case of **the subverter** listed among those liable to be executed by stoning, **this is one who says: Let us go and worship idols. And Rav Yehuda says** that **Rav says:** In this mishna the Sages **taught** the case of **the subverters of an idolatrous city.** Here **we arrive at** the opinion of **the Rabbis,** who hold that those who incite a multitude of people are also executed by stoning. Is it possible that **the first clause** of the mishna expresses the opinion of **Rabbi Shimon, and the last clause** expresses that of **the Rabbis?**

Ravina says: The entire mishna **is** in accordance with the opinion of **the Rabbis, and** the *tanna* **teaches** the mishna employing the style of: **Not** only **this** but **also that.** In other words, the mishna should be explained as follows: Not only is one who incites an individual executed by stoning, but even one who subverts an entire city is executed by stoning.

Rav Pappa says: When the mishna **teaches** with regard to one who **incites** that **this is** referring to **an ordinary person,** it is not indicating that a prophet is not included in this *halakha*. Rather, it is referring **to the hiding** of witnesses behind a fence in order to ensnare the inciter, as his life is treated with contempt and derision, as though he were an ordinary person, i.e., a simpleton.

As it is taught in a *baraita*: **And** with regard to **all the rest of those liable to** receive the **death** penalty **by Torah** law, the court **does not hide** witnesses in order **to** ensnare **them** and punish them **except for this** case of an inciter.

How does the court **do** this **to him?** The agents of the court **light a candle for him in an inner room, and** they **place witnesses for him in an outer room** in the dark, **so that they can see him and hear his voice but he cannot see them. And the other** person, whom the inciter had previously tried to incite, **says to him: Say what you said to me** when we were **in seclusion. And he says to him** again that he should worship the idol. **And the other** person **says to him: How can we forsake our God in Heaven and worship idols?** If the inciter **retracts** his suggestion, **that is good. But if he says: This** idol worship **is our duty, and this** is what **suits us, the witnesses, who are listening from outside, bring him to court, and** they **have him stoned.**

And the court **did the same to** an inciter named **ben Setada**[3], **from** the city of **Lod, and they hanged him on Passover eve.**

The Gemara asks: Why did they call him **ben Setada,** when **he was the son of Pandeira? Rav Ḥisda says:** Perhaps his mother's **husband,** who acted as his father, was named **Setada,** but his mother's **paramour,** who fathered this *mamzer*, was named **Pandeira.** The Gemara challenges: But his mother's **husband was Pappos ben Yehuda,** not Setada. **Rather,** perhaps **his mother** was named **Setada,** and he was named ben Setada after her. The Gemara challenges: But **his mother was Miriam, who braided women's hair.** The Gemara explains: That is not a contradiction; Setada was

---

3. The name can be vocalized in one of two ways, Stada or Setada.

merely a nickname, **as they say in Pumbedita: This one strayed** [setat da] **from her husband.**

The charges against Jesus the Nazarene were serious, capital offenses: sorcery and being an inciter to idolatry. As Maimonides said much later, "the entire Torah is oriented towards the struggle against idolatry" (*Guide for the Perplexed* 3:29). To give an idea of comparable offenses in the Talmud consider the following:

> *Sanhedrin 53a*
> MISHNA: **These** transgressors **are those who are stoned** to death: **One who engages in intercourse with** his **mother; or with** his **father's wife,** even if she is not his mother; **or with** his **daughter-in-law; or with a male; or with an animal; and a woman who engages in intercourse with an animal. And one who blasphemes, and one who engages in idol worship. And one who gives of his offspring to Molekh, and a necromancer, and a sorcerer. And one who desecrates Shabbat, and one who curses his father or his mother, and one who engages in intercourse with a betrothed young woman, and an inciter** who incites individuals to idol worship, **and a subverter** who incites an entire city to idol worship, **and a warlock, and a stubborn and rebellious son.**

The prohibition of being a *mesit*, an inciter is an especially serious crime under Torah law:

> *Deuteronomy 13:7–9*
> If your brother, your own mother's son," or your son or daughter, or the wife of your bosom, or your closest friend" entices you in secret, saying, "Come let us worship other gods"—whom neither you nor your ancestors have experienced. —from among the gods of the peoples around you, either near to you or distant, anywhere from one end of the earth to the other: do not assent or give heed to any of them. Show no pity or compassion, and do not cover up the matter

The category of *mesit* under rabbinic law implies deceiving a large number of people, indicating that the Rabbis considered Jesus to have had a successful career in influencing regular people in his teachings.

> *Sanhedrin 67a*
> MISHNA: With regard to the case of **an inciter,** listed among those liable to be executed by stoning, **this is an ordinary person,** not a prophet. **And** it is referring to **one who incites an ordinary**

person and not a multitude of people. What does the inciter do? **He says: There is an idol in such and such a place,** which **eats like this, drinks like this, does good** for its worshippers **like this,** and **harms** those who do not worship it **like this.**

The mishna states a principle with regard to the *halakha* of an inciter: With regard to **all of those** mentioned **in the Torah** who **are liable to** receive **the death** penalty, if there are no witnesses to their transgressions, the court **does not hide** witnesses in order **to** ensnare and punish **them, except for this** case of an inciter.

The mishna elaborates: If the inciter **said** his words of incitement **to two** men, **they are his witnesses, and** he does not need to be warned before the transgression; **they bring him to court and stone him.** If **he said** his words of incitement **to one** man alone, that man's testimony would not be sufficient to have the inciter executed. Therefore **he says** to the inciter: **I have friends who are interested in this;** tell them too. This way there will be more witnesses.

Other texts recognize the severity of the charges.[4]

Jesus broke from his teacher and the rest of the rabbis at some point during his studies and likely in Egypt. He began to teach in Israel and, apparently, had great success, but he was excommunicated by his teacher and later arrested by the Sanhedrin. The charges brought against Jesus are plainly stated: Jesus the Nazarene is going out to be stoned because he practiced sorcery, incited people to idol worship, and led the Jewish people astray (Sanhedrin 43a).

"Practicing sorcery" is a reference to the use of magic in healing. Jesus was a well-known healer, using magical techniques to cure the masses throughout Judea and Galilee. His name was used in magical spells after his death to cure various illnesses. This was *not* prohibited in rabbinic or Pharisaic Judaism, *if* the technique was acceptable to the religious authorities but, in Jesus' case, I propose that his use of saliva as a healing technique was *not* acceptable to Jewish religious authorities of the time.

"Incited people to idol worship" is harder to pin down exactly, although I think there are clues. To learn more, we must turn to the Gospels and the story of the Cleansing of the Temple.[5] This tradition is likely authentic, because it is shared by all four Gospels. Looking at the version in Mark, we see,

4. Sanhedrin 61a, 84b, 89a

5. Matthew 21:12–13; Mark 11:15–19; Luke 19:45–48; John 2:13–22

"Then they came to Jerusalem. And he entered the temple and began to drive out those who were selling and those who were buying in the temple, and he overturned the tables of the money changers and the seats of those who sold doves, and he would not allow anyone to carry anything through the temple. He was teaching and saying, "Is it not written: 'My house shall be called a house of prayer for all the nations'? But you have made it a den of robbers.""

The presence of moneychangers and sellers was *necessary* for the proper functioning of the Temple, which housed worshipers from around the Jewish world, who needed to exchange their currency for local currency. They would also need to acquire animals to bring for a sacrifice. There are a multitude of ways to interpret the incident in the Gospels, but it must remain at the forefront that this was an attack on the centralized house of Jewish worship. Neusner read this as a transgressive action that began the process of separation between Judaism and Christianity, a reading which is in line with the rabbinic texts themselves, placing the blame for the separation between the religions on Jesus himself, rather than Paul, as modern scholars might do. This was an act that showed Jesus' rejection of the Temple cult as a means of atonement.

Idolatry is a bad translation of the Hebrew *avodah zarah*, which means 'foreign worship.' This certainly includes worship of other gods besides the God of the Hebrew Bible or even worship of lesser spiritual beings, such as angels. However, it also includes illicit worship of the true God. To protest against the divinely ordained cult was equated with *avodah zarah*, "foreign worship" because it introduced a new way to worship God that was not sanctioned by the Torah.[6] *Inciting* people to idolatry was a serious prohibition, as we saw earlier. This must refer to Jesus' teaching, which must have included an anti-Temple cult element, perhaps relying on the verses from Isaiah 56:7 (house of prayer for all nations) and Jeremiah 7:11 (den of robbers). While there was a strain of anti-sacrifice theology among the Jewish prophets, Jesus seems to have taken this to its ultimate conclusion, to reject the sacrificial cult as a means of atonement, and teaching others the same.

---

6. It is true that the Rabbis later decided to shift the focus of Judaism from the Temple to prayer and study of Torah. However, this occurred *after* the destruction of the Temple in 70 CE.

This was a step too far for the religious authorities in Jerusalem. The religious establishment likely feared a revolt and proceeded to go forward with the arrest and trial of Jesus.[7]

How does this fit with the Christian narrative?

The Gospels present two charges: blasphemy because Jesus pretended to be the Messiah, and, therefore, in Christian understanding, to be the Son of God. Pilate understands Jesus to want to be the king of the Jews and a political rebel. Idolatry is equated with blasphemy in other passages (Mishnah Sanhedrin 6:4, 7:4). While the New Testament does not mention the charge of sorcery, Jesus' claim to destroy the Temple and rebuild it in three days (Mark 14:58; John 2:19) might be understood as sorcery. "Moreover, Jesus' practice of casting out demons is explicitly connected with the messianic claim and may indeed be pre- supposed in the trial before the High Court. Interestingly enough, when Celsus portrays Jesus as returning with "certain magical powers" from Egypt, he concludes that "because of these powers, and on account of them [he] gave himself the title of God," clearly connecting sorcery with the claim to be God. It is futile, therefore, to contrast too narrowly the charge of blasphemy (New Testament) with the charge of idolatry/sorcery (Bavli)."[8]

7. Sanders, *Jesus*, 1993.

8. Schäfer, *Jesus in the Talmud* p. 68,

What Happened after Jesus' Death?

W HAT HAPPENED AFTER JESUS' death?
        We cannot know with any certainty.

Taking into account the Talmud's chronology, we can speculate about the emergence of New Testament communities. It is likely that there was some split among his followers after his death. The Talmud does not mention Jesus as a messianic claimant and does not attribute to him any of the characteristics of messianic claimants of the time. He is presented as a *rabbi*, albeit a heretical one. His teaching is like that of the Rabbis, and he is a (former) member of the top echelons of rabbinic society, being the student of the *nasi*. It is true that the Rabbis of the Talmud are uncomfortable with messianism and avoid the subject, but there is little evidence that they considered Jesus as a messianic claimant. Their issue with Jesus was his use of magic and his opposition to the cult of the Temple. It also seems that most messianic movements died with their founders.[1]

Jesus' teaching is not preserved well in the Talmud. However, we learn that Jesus did have *halakhic* teachings.[2] His teachings were recorded in the *avon gilyon*, as the Rabbis knew it.[3] He likely shared in the highly spiritual cosmology of the time. Jesus refers to the Son of Man figure in the

1. It is possible that Jesus used magic and miraculous deeds to present his case as a messianic claimant, such as Theudas and the Egyptian had done.

2. Some interpret Jesus' teaching on the Sabbath and divorce as halakhic teachings in the Gospel of Matthew, see Sigal, *The Halakhah of Jesus*.

3. Some would argue that the Rabbis had and preserved a Hebrew copy of Matthew, see Howard, *The Hebrew Gospel*.

Gospels, which was some sort of angelic being, identified with either the angel Michael or the heavenly hosts of angelic beings (called "saints"). Jesus *might* have also shared in the apocalypticism of the day, beginning (textually) in Daniel, composed during the time of Antiochus IV Epiphanes, in which the universe was viewed as comprising of the heavens above and the earth below, where heavenly events above could be mirrored in the earth.[4] Even if Jesus and his followers did not originally subscribe to these ideas, later Christians did.

If Jesus lived in the first century BCE[5], then his teachings would have circulated for some time before the development of what we now call the early Church. There has always been a strong identification of Christianity with the Diaspora, with only the Jerusalem community under Jacob (James) existing in the Holy Land itself. It is likely that followers of Jesus in

4. Collins, "The Son of Man."

5. It is possible that the Talmudic chronology is based on a misattribution. The doublet tradition in the Bavli (Sotah 47a; Sanhedrin 107b) about Jesus and his teacher, Yehoshua, at the inn, is preserved in the Jerusalem Talmud (Ḥagigah 2:2), where Yehudah ben Tabbai's student is the one who misunderstood him (see page 113). Misattribution of traditions was a common problem in the Babylonian Talmud: "The dictum that "one who says something in the name of the one who stated it brings redemption to the world" [M Avot 6:6; BT Meg 15a; Hul 104b; Nid 19b; Kallah 1:1; Kallah 8:1] motivated the collection of variant attributions and other traditions. The Bavli contains over 750 cases in which alternate attributions are given . . . [T]he variant attributions can often be understood as possibilities arising from the vagaries of association, where the Amoraic statement is attributed to contemporaries who are closely associated, as in the case of R. Yohanan and his close disciple, R. Abbahu (Pes 100a), or when the two names can easily be aurally confused, as in the case of R. Abin and R. Abina (Ber 7a) or R. Ahali and R. Yehiel (Erub 12a), or when one element of a name is common to both, as in the case of R. Yose b. Abin and R. Yose b. Zevida (Ber 13a) or R. Levi b. Hamma and R. Hamma b. Hanina (Suk 47a). These alternatives are such as might have occurred either in the process of oral transmission, or there is reason to believe that one authority had actually quoted the other. (Elman 1999, pp. 61–62).

The misattribution could be based on the phonetic approximation between the three names: *Yehoshua; Yehudah; Yeshua* (ישוע, יהודה, יהושע). It is likely that the link between Yehoshua and Yehudah (ben Tabbai) was the original teacher-disciple tradition, which is maintained in Pirke Avot's list of the transmission of the oral tradition (1:8). This fits into the tradition of *zugot* ("pairs") of that part of the chain. Yehoshua ben Perachiah and Nittai the Arbelite pass the tradition to Shimon ben Shetach and Yehudah ben Tabbai. The addition of a third prominent student, Yeshu ben Pantera, distorts the "pairs' tradition and contradicts earlier sources. It is also possible that the Rabbis were in contact with a Christian group who followed the 1st century BCE timeline, as preserved in Epiphanius' *Panarion* (Carrier 2014, pp. 281ff) or, the Babylonian Rabbis associated Yehoshua ben Peraḥiah and Jesus through magic, due to the occurrence of both names on magical incantation bowls (Schäfer 2007, p. 38–39.

the Diaspora began to have visions of Jesus in heaven, perhaps beginning with Paul.

While a small nucleus of the movement remained in Judea, becoming one of the minor Jewish sects of that time, the greatest gains were made in the Diaspora, in Antioch, Alexandria, and throughout the Greco-Roman world, where Jesus' ideas could take root and develop. Paul was a follower of Jesus, who joined the movement after opposing it (Galatians 1–2). He began to have visions of Jesus as the Messiah, a term not applied to Jesus before Paul. Jesus' name means 'salvation' and was a common name among messianic groups of the time.[6]

Two tracks began to develop in the Jesus movement in the first century CE, one in the Diaspora, spearheaded by Paul, and another in Jerusalem, under Jacob (James). Paul begins to identify Jesus as the messiah and maintains that his death was a means of atonement. This supplements Jesus' own anti-sacrificial mentality. Now, Jesus' death *replaces* the Temple as the means of atonement. Meanwhile, in Jerusalem, Jacob, Cephas and John must have interacted with members of John the Baptist's movement and the Qumran group. All Jews became more apocalyptic in the first century CE, and Jesus' followers were no exception. Perhaps the changing political situation also created a sense of apocalyptic urgency that was not present in Jesus' original teaching. It might also be the case that his followers in Jerusalem began to think of him as some form of exalted teacher, like the Teacher of Righteousness, of the Qumran community. It is easy to see how, after his death, this could have been developed into some form of messianic thought.

Paul does not know any of the stories of Jesus as found in the later Gospels, implying that some or most of those stories are either invented or come from different communities than his. For Paul, the entire message of Jesus is his atoning death, called the *gospel*, or "proclamation." Paul sees himself as a "messenger to the Gentiles" proclaiming the messianic kingdom of Jesus, who he has seen in visions. In Galatians, he reports that he met with Cephas (Peter), Jacob (James) and John, and they eventually sanctioned his "mission to the Gentiles", but it is not entirely clear how accurate that picture is. He seems to have regarded Jesus' historical life as of little value, placing much more value on the risen Christ, whose death provided a means of forgiveness of sins for humankind.

---

6. This section is influenced by the theories in Ellegard. *Jesus.*

This Pauline group began to spread among the Jews and Gentiles, particularly the latter. They must have interacted with the Jerusalem Community and Ebionite communities. These were a spectrum of viewpoints about Jesus, the Law, and Gnosticism, with varying degrees of proto-rabbinic orthodoxy. The Paulines became part of the proto-orthodox camp as well as the Marcionites, and there were countless other iterations of the Jesus movement along a Marcionite-Ebionite spectrum.

Paul's communities began to write their own stories, culminating in the Gospel of Mark, which recounts the origin of Paul's "announcement" (*gospel*). They had traditions of the death and resurrection of Jesus and that he was a miracle worker. Some of Paul's teachings were reworked into the Gospel as Jesus' teachings. Mark's Gospel is a bare-bones structure to provide some historical context to Paul's announcement, while Matthew and Luke's communities were at different points on the continuum and wrote Gospels to counter Mark's Gospel, but accepted his basic structure; this made them easier to integrate into the proto-orthodox canon.[7]

Therefore, the development of Christianity began from pre-Christian Gnosticism in Jewish circles, which must have been taught by Jesus during his earthly life in the first century BCE. As time progressed, a group of Judeo-Christians, called Ebionites began to follow in Jesus' legacy and presented a collection of sayings, now known by scholars as Q. This tradition followed in Jesus' Gnostic teachings and later adopted the structure of the Pauline Gospel to tell its own stories.

As the Jews' political fate waned with the two unsuccessful rebellions against Rome, the Ebionite and other Judeo-Christian communities began to disappear. This provided the moment for the proto-orthodox to ascend, as they could refashion the Jewish scriptures as part of their own story and the developing replacement theology that would eventually become the official doctrine of the Church.

At the same time, the Rabbis began to define their own community in the post-Temple era, as the natural center of the Jewish people disappeared. The Rabbis began to reconstruct the story of Israel and their own role as they became the sole survivors of Second Temple Judaism. They seemed to be related to the Pharisees in some way, but sought to recast their legacy as non-denominational, in a sense, and as representing the only valid expression of Judaism throughout history. It was at this time that the stories of Yeshua ben Pantera were recast as well. Before this moment, Jesus would have

---

7. Dykstra, *Mark Canonizer of Paul.*

been still considered a Jew, but not a *ḥaver*, part of the Pharisaic-rabbinic community.[8] The Rabbis began to distance themselves from Gnosticism and magic. They also saw that the nascent Christian community had begun to refashion the stories of Jesus to suit their own needs. The Rabbis wanted to avoid sectarianism to project their own community as *de facto*, "Israel." They began to reject Jesus and Judeo-Christians from their own story of Israel, but it is uncertain if the traditions of Jesus being excommunicated are from the age of Yehoshua ben Peraḥyah or if they were invented (or exaggerated) at the time of their separation from the Judeo-Christians. There is a similar effort to excommunicate and erase other figures associated with magic in the proto-rabbinic community. Their memory is not found in the main tannaitic work, the Mishnah, but can be found in trace samples in the Tosefta.

The Gospels both create new memories and project aspects of Paul's life and teaching onto "Jesus of Nazareth," as well as using Greco-Roman historiographical tropes and the Hebrew Scriptures as source material.[9] It is possible that the Gospels also preserve some basic memories of Jesus the Nazarene. However, there is little connection between them and the Jesus communities that succeeded him. It seems that the entirety of Paul's connection to the historical Jesus and the historical Jesus movement is tangential at best, but more realistically non-existent.

Both Paul and Jesus and most of everyone else in the ancient world believed in magic. This continued to be the case for most people throughout most of human history, even until modern times. You can find examples of this with many common ideas, such as instant karma, going outside will catch a cold, various home remedies, and much more. These are all remnants of a more robust, magical thinking that existed in all human societies. However, both the Rabbis and the Church Fathers wanted to minimize the use of magic within their orthodox circles.

So, Jesus was lost to Jewish history, either by his own actions or those of the generations that succeeded him, or perhaps, both. It could have been a result of the decision of his own teachers or due to the political agenda of the Rabbis. What is true is that he was erased from the memory of the rabbinic community. All that remains now is a faint memory of a man who

---

8. Some doubt that the Pharisees were related to the proto-rabbis at all, instead drawing a line from the community of scribes developed after the post-Exilic period, including Ben Sira, to the Rabbis. See Sigal, *The Halakhah of Jesus*.

9. Dykstra, *Mark Canonizer of Paul*.

existed at one point. And perhaps, a body. Yes, there is an obscure reference from *much* later, from Rabbi Isaac Luria who lived in Safed in Israel. He notes,

> *Rabbi Isaac Luria, Book of Reincarnations, Chapter 37*
> "On your way from Safed toward the North to the village of Ein al-Zeitun, passing a carob tree, Yeshu Ha-Notzri is buried there."

This is a presentation of the life of Jesus according to the rabbinic sources, with a healthy bit of speculation on my part.

Jesus' Followers and the Early Christian Movement

J ESUS DIED, AS ALL do, but his ideas lived on. How did Jesus' ideas become a major world religion? This is only a brief treatment of his direct successors, the Judeo-Christians, who existed in a number of different forms after his death. However, they are as much a part of his story in the Talmud, because it is through the *minim* ('heretics') that we learn about Jesus himself.

Jesus was a charismatic teacher and healer. He likely did not set up any organization or mechanism to continue his movement after his death. What existed was a collection of teachings and a technique for magical healing, and his followers continued with these two things and perpetuated his name for years after his death. Unfortunately, all of the information we have about the Judeo-Christians is from Christian heresiologists, who are not known for historical accuracy. However, this is all the information that we have. Therefore, we will explore what we know about Jesus' followers after his death.

The Ebionites are referenced in several places throughout the Church Fathers. One of the earlier references is from one of Justin Martyr's surviving works. Justin was born in Samaria in 100 CE, as the separation between Judaism and Christianity was continuing to develop. He was not Jewish and seems to have converted to Christianity at some point in his life, after meeting a Christian who convinced him of the truth of Jesus. He renounced his philosophical background and former religion and joined the Church, meaning the proto-orthodox movement of Christians who synthesized

Marcionism, Paulinism, and Ebionism. The reference to the Ebionites is found in *Dialogue with Trypho*[1] from around 150 CE, in which a conversation with Trypho, a Jew, is recorded and Justin convinces him of the truth of the Christian religion.

The specific portion here begins when Trypho asks a question about Christians who choose to observe the Law. Justin indicates that he thinks these men will be saved, if they do not convince others to follow in their error (according to Justin), although there are others who do not agree with Justin and think that these men will not be saved. Justin attributes this to weakness in faith in Christ, but allows people to observe if they must. He explains that his Christian group believes that the Law was given out of "the hardness of the people's hearts" and not out of "virtue" as the Judeo-Christians believe. There is later discussion of essentially keeping this to oneself if one must observe the Law. However, Justin indicates that non-believing Jews will not be saved and especially those who "anathematize this very Christ in the synagogues" will not be saved.

> *Justin Dialogue with Trypho Chapter 47*
> *Trypho:* But if some one, knowing that this is so, after he recognises that this man is Christ, and has believed in and obeys Him, wishes, however, to observe these [institutions], will he be saved?
> *Justin:* In my opinion, Trypho, such an one will be saved, if he does not strive in every way to persuade other men — I mean those Gentiles who have been circumcised from error by Christ, to observe the same things as himself, telling them that they will not be saved unless they do so. This you did yourself at the commencement of the discourse, when you declared that I would not be saved unless I observe these institutions.
> *Trypho:* Why then have you said, 'In my opinion, such an one will be saved,' unless there are some who affirm that such will not be saved?
> *Justin:* There are such people, Trypho, and these do not venture to have any intercourse with or to extend hospitality to such persons; but I do not agree with them. But if some, through weak-mindedness, wish to observe such institutions as were given by Moses, from which they expect some virtue, but which we believe were appointed by reason of the hardness of the people's hearts, along with their hope in this Christ, and [wish to perform] the eternal and natural acts of righteousness and piety, yet choose to

---

1. There is some speculation that "Trypho" is Rabbi Tarfon, from Lod, the same city as Jesus was in the Talmud, who interacted frequently with Judeo-Christians.

live with the Christians and the faithful, as I said before, not in-ducing them either to be circumcised like themselves, or to keep the Sabbath, or to observe any other such ceremonies, then I hold that we ought to join ourselves to such, and associate with them in all things as kinsmen and brethren. But if, Trypho, some of your race, who say they believe in this Christ, compel those Gentiles who believe in this Christ to live in all respects according to the law given by Moses, or choose not to associate so intimately with them, I in like manner do not approve of them. But I believe that even those, who have been persuaded by them to observe the legal dispensation along with their confession of God in Christ, shall probably be saved. And I hold, further, that such as have confessed and known this man to be Christ, yet who have gone back from some cause to the legal dispensation, and have denied that this man is Christ, and have repented not before death, shall by no means be saved. Further, I hold that those of the seed of Abraham who live according to the law, and do not believe in this Christ before death, shall likewise not be saved, and especially those who have anathematized and do anathematize this very Christ in the synagogues, and everything by which they might obtain salvation and escape the vengeance of fire. For the goodness and the loving-kindness of God, and His boundless riches, hold righteous and sinless the man who, as Ezekiel tells, repents of sins; and reckons sinful, unrighteous, and impious the man who fails away from piety and righteousness to unrighteousness and ungodliness. Wherefore also our Lord Jesus Christ said, 'In whatsoever things I shall take you, in these I shall judge you.'

The text from Justin is interesting not because of the information it provides about the Ebionites, for it provides next to nothing, but rather to understand the social dynamic between Jews and Christians in his time, which must have still been fluid. There was growing antagonism between the groups but still a gray middle zone. It seems there was also still move-ment in both directions, i.e. Jews who became Christian and Christians who became Jews.

A more explicit reference to Ebionites is found in Irenaeus' famous work, *Against Heresies*. Irenaeus himself was from Smyrna in Asia Minor and born around 130 CE. After persecution in Asia Minor, he became a priest and later bishop in southern France. He writes about the Ebionites but in an indirect manner as well. He refers to the heresy of Cerinthus, who was later associated with the Ebionites by later Church historians. Cerinthus would have been born around 50 CE and active in the second half of the 1st century. He is lumped with the Ebionites for having a similar Christology.

What was his view of Christ? He believed that Jesus was a natural son of Joseph and Mary, as the Ebionites believed (at least some of them). Cerinthus is accused of being educated in the "wisdom of the Egyptians" which must imply some sort of Gnostic training and belief. Ireneaeus then describes the nature of his heresy. He believed that God did not create the world but used a "Power" separated from him, similar to all Gnostic theology. Jesus was a supremely righteous man, more so than any man in his generation. After his baptism, the spiritual Christ descended into the man Jesus and through this spiritual Christ, Jesus performed miracles. The spiritual Christ left Jesus at his death (but Jesus still died and rose again).

Irenaeus then mentions the Ebionites, noting their similar Christology. He then adds that the Ebionites only use the Gospel of Matthew and repudiate the Apostle Paul. The Ebionites did not regard Paul as an apostle but as a proselyte to Judaism who distorted Jesus' teachings. Irenaeus notes something of the Ebionites interpretations of the Prophets, although it is not clear what is meant in the passage and that they observe Jewish law as other Jews would.

Irenaeus, Against Heresies 1:26

Cerinthus, again, a man who was educated in the wisdom of the Egyptians, taught that the world was not made by the primary God, but by a certain Power far separated from him, and at a distance from that Principality who is supreme over the universe, and ignorant of him who is above all. He represented Jesus as having not been born of a virgin, but as being the son of Joseph and Mary according to the ordinary course of human generation, while he nevertheless was more righteous, prudent, and wise than other men. Moreover, after his baptism, Christ descended upon him in the form of a dove from the Supreme Ruler, and that then he proclaimed the unknown Father, and performed miracles. But at last Christ departed from Jesus, and that then Jesus suffered and rose again, while Christ remained impassible, inasmuch as he was a spiritual being.

Those who are called Ebionites agree that the world was made by God; but their opinions with respect to the Lord are similar to those of Cerinthus and Carpocrates. They use the Gospel according to Matthew only, and repudiate the Apostle Paul, maintaining that he was an apostate from the law. As to the prophetical writings, they endeavor to expound them in a somewhat singular manner: they practice circumcision, persevere in the observance of those customs which are enjoined by the law, and are so Judaic in their style of life, that they even adore Jerusalem as if it were the house of God.

Irenaeus mentions the Ebionites in another part of his work. In this section, he is expounding on the text in Isaiah 7:14 and the translation of the word for *young woman* which is translated differently between Greek and Hebrew. He notes that some Jewish proselytes interpret this as a young *woman* not *virgin* in the manner of the Ebionites.

Irenaeus, Against Heresies 3:21
God, then, was made man, and the Lord did Himself save us, giving us the token of the Virgin. But not as some allege, among those now presuming to expound the Scripture, [thus:] *Behold, a young woman shall conceive, and bring forth a son,* Isaiah 7:14 as Theodotion the Ephesian has interpreted, and Aquila of Pontus, both Jewish proselytes. The Ebionites, following these, assert that He was begotten by Joseph; thus destroying, as far as in them lies, such a marvelous dispensation of God, and setting aside the testimony of the prophets which proceeded from God. For truly this prediction was uttered before the removal of the people to Babylon; that is, anterior to the supremacy acquired by the Medes and Persians. But it was interpreted into Greek by the Jews themselves, much before the period of our Lord's advent, that there might remain no suspicion that perchance the Jews, complying with our humor, did put this interpretation upon these words. They indeed, had they been cognizant of our future existence, and that we should use these proofs from the Scriptures, would themselves never have hesitated to burn their own Scriptures, which do declare that all other nations partake of [eternal] life, and show that they who boast themselves as being the house of Jacob and the people of Israel, are disinherited from the grace of God.

By far, the *Panarion* by Epiphanius of Salamis is the work that provides the most information about the Ebionites and other Judeo-Christians. Epiphanius seems to have been a Romaniote (Greek-speaking) Jew born near Eleutheropolis in Palestine, southwest of Jerusalem. He spoke several languages, including Hebrew, Syriac, Egyptian, Greek and Latin. He became a Christian priest and was later consecrated as the bishop of Cyprus around 365 CE. His work, *The Panarion*, provides information on eighty different "heretical" sects of his day.

Epiphanius presents the founder of the Ebionites as being Ebion, one of the Nazoraeans' school of thought, but he taught different things than they did. He also seems to think that Ebion was a Samaritan.

> *Panarion 30 2:8*
> And as far as I know, he first lived in a village called Cocabe in the district of Qarnaim—also called Ashtaroth—in Bashanitis. There he began his evil teaching—the place, if you please, where the Nazoraeans I have spoken of came from.

Most scholars doubt there was a man named Ebion and instead tie this to the Hebrew word *evyon*, meaning "poor". This is attested by Eusebius:

> *Eusebius Historia Eclesiastica 3.27.6*
> Wherefore, in consequence of such a course they received the name of Ebionites, which signified the poverty of their understanding. For this is the name by which a poor man is called among the Hebrews.

This association gives new meaning to Paul's agreement with the Jerusalem leaders in Galatians.

> *Galatians 2:9–10*
> and when James and Cephas and John, who were acknowledged pillars, recognized the grace that had been given to me, they gave to Barnabas and me the right hand of fellowship, agreeing that we should go to the Gentiles and they to the circumcised. They asked only one thing, *that we remember the poor*, which was actually what I was eager to do.

Perhaps this also has some connection to one of the Beatitudes, "Blessed are the poor in spirit, for theirs is the kingdom of heaven" (Matt. 5:3)? One can only wonder at the potential allusions throughout the New Testament to real people and places.

What did the Ebionites teach? First, they agreed with other sects that "Christ was conceived by sexual intercourse and the seed of a man, Joseph" but Ebion was different because of "his adherence to Judaism's Law of the Sabbath, circumcision, and all the other Jewish and Samaritan observances" (Panarion 30 2:2). The man Jesus was a common man, even poor among the Jews, but was rewarded for his righteousness, in the most common version of Ebionite Christology (Eusebius *Historia Eclesiastica* 3 27.2). There was a variety of opinions among the Ebionites though, as not all agreed with this teaching of Christ's origin as the natural offspring of Mary and

Joseph, "For some of them even say that Adam is Christ—the man who was formed first and infused with God's breath" (*Panarion* 30 3:3). What this means isn't exactly clear but it must be related to the various comparisons between Jesus and Adam in the New Testament. Yet, other Ebionites had different views altogether:

> *Panarion 30 3:4*
> But others among them say that he is from above; created before all things, a spirit, both higher than the angels and Lord of all; and that he is called Christ, the heir of the world there. But he comes here when he chooses, as he came in Adam and appeared to the patriarchs clothed with Adam's body. And in the last days the same Christ who had come to Abraham, Isaac and Jacob, came and donned Adam's body, and appeared to men, was crucified, rose and ascended.

This fits with the spiritual Christ theory that Christ was identified with the Metatron and Son of Man, a preexistent spiritual being that could descend into historical people. Some Ebionites believed that Christ descended into multiple people, including the historical Jesus (*Panarion* 30 3:6).

Yet, there were others who seemed to hold to the proto-orthodox view:

> *Origen Contra Celsum 5.61*
> and these are the twofold sect of Ebionites, who either acknowledge with us that Jesus was born of a virgin, or deny this, and maintain that He was begotten like other human beings

However, their beliefs were not entirely congruent with the proto-orthodox:

> *Eusebius Historia Eclesiastica 3 27.3*
> 3. There were others, however, besides them, that were of the same name, but avoided the strange and absurd beliefs of the former, and did not deny that the Lord was born of a virgin and of the Holy Spirit. But nevertheless, inasmuch as they also refused to acknowledge that he pre-existed, being God, Word, and Wisdom, they turned aside into the impiety of the former, especially when they, like them, endeavored to observe strictly the bodily worship of the law.

Some Ebionites had a strict interpretation of Jewish law, even more so than the proto-rabbis. Epiphanius records that "Ebion" prohibited touching gentiles, in the manner of the Samaritans (*Panarion* 30 2:3). Likewise, if a man had been intimate with a woman, he needed to immerse in water (*Panarion* 30 2:4). The Ebionites in Epiphanius' account show evolution from earlier times, as one would expect. They prided themselves on their virginity in earlier times. Epiphanius thinks this is in imitation of James, "the Lord's brother", who didn't marry. However, in his day, they forbid celibacy and continence (*Panarion* 30 2:6).

The Ebionites had a version of the Gospel of Matthew, which they alone regarded as Scripture, from the New Testament canon. This was written in Hebrew and is one of the lost Hebrew Gospels (*Panarion* 30 3:7). Epiphanius says that they also use the Gospel of John, translated from Greek to Hebrew and that they have copies of these Gospels in a geniza in Tiberias (*Panarion* 30 3:8). The Ebionites had other writings too. The Travels of Peter, written by Clement (*Panarion* 30 15:1) and other Clementine literature, as well as the Ascent of James (*Panarion* 30 16:7).

The Ebionites' Matthew is not the same as the canonical Matthew. Epiphanius makes sure we know that it is heretical. The changes relate to the Ebionites' view of Jesus, starting with the very beginning. The Cerinthians and other groups with similar views use the genealogy at the beginning of the Gospel to prove that Jesus was the natural offspring of Mary and Joseph (*Panarion* 30 14:2). The opening of the Ebionite Gospel is as follows:

> *Panarion 30 14:3*
> But these people have something else in mind. They falsify the genealogical tables in *Matthew's Gospel* and make its opening, as I said, 'It came to pass in the days of Herod, king of Judea, in the high-priesthood of Caiaphas, that a certain man, John by name, came baptizing with the baptism of repentance in the river Jordan' and so on.

This fits with Ebionite Christology because they view Jesus and Christ as two separate entities. Jesus is the man who led a righteous life and was used by God. The Christ is a pre-existent spiritual energy that can inhabit human beings (*Panarion* 30 14:4). They held strongly dualistic views, thinking that the devil and the Christ were appointed by God, the Christ was given the world to come and the devil the current, material world (*Panarion* 30 16:2). Jesus was God's chosen representative on earth, meriting to be inhabited by the Christ from on high (*Panarion* 30 16:3). The Christ is the highest of the angels and archangels and the highest creature of God, *but not equal to God* (*Panarion* 30 16:4). The Christ came to Jesus with the explicit purpose of abolishing the animal sacrifices in the Temple, likely a too 'material' form of worship for the Ebionites. The Ebionite Gospel says that Jesus himself said, "I came to abolish the sacrifices, and if ye cease not from sacrifice, wrath will not cease from you" (*Panarion* 30 16:5). This is a theme throughout Ebionite literature.[2]

The Ebionites were opposed to the Paulines and to the Apostle Paul himself. They also opposed the Church history found in Luke-Acts (*Panarion* 30 16:6). Epiphanius records their thoughts on the Apostle himself:

> *Panarion 30 16:8–9*
> Nor are they ashamed to accuse Paul here with certain fabrications of their false apostles' villainy and imposture. They say that he was Tarsean—which he admits himself and does not deny. And they suppose that he was of Greek parentage, taking the occasion for this from the (same) passage because of his frank statement, 'I am a man of Tarsus, a citizen of no mean city.' They then claim that he was Greek and the son of a Greek mother and Greek father, but that he had gone up to Jerusalem, stayed there for a while, desired to marry a daughter of the high priest, and had therefore became a proselyte and been circumcised. But since he still could not marry that sort of girl he became angry and wrote against circumcision, and against the Sabbath and the legislation (cf. Eusebius *Historia Eclesiastica* 3 27.4).

It seems that the "false gospel" Paul was battling in Galatians might have been the proto-Ebionites themselves. Epiphanius records that they preached in Asia and Rome, although their strength seemed to be in Syria and Arabia[3] (*Panarion* 30 18:1).

Great effort is made to paint a picture of the Jewishness of the Ebionites, for example:

> *Origen Contra Celsum 5.61*
> Let it be admitted, moreover, that there are some who accept Jesus, and who boast on that account of being Christians, and yet would regulate their lives, like the Jewish multitude, in accordance with the Jewish law

Although Epiphanius and others go to great lengths to show that the Ebionites were thoroughly Jewish, their doctrine and practice did deviate from proto-rabbinic Judaism in several important ways. First, they engaged in baptism and daily baptism, presumably two different rituals. They also

---

2. *Clementine Homilies* 2.44.2; 3.26.3; 3.45.1–2; 56.4, and *Recognitions* 1.37 1.39.12

3. Coincidentally, this is where Paul began his movement (Galatians 1–2).

had a "eucharistic" ceremony with unleavened bread and water (*Panarion* 30 16:1). They called their places of worship "synagogues" and had elders and synagogue presidents (*Panarion* 30 18:2). They seemed to celebrate *both* the Jewish Sabbath and the Christian "Lord's Day":

> *Eusebius Historia Eclesiastica 3.27.5*
> The Sabbath and the rest of the discipline of the Jews they observed just like them, but at the same time, like us, they celebrated the Lord's days as a memorial of the resurrection of the Savior.

However, they seemed to have a permissive view of divorce, following the essentially same halakhah as the Rabbis (*Panarion* 30 18:3). With other Jews, they acknowledged the Patriarchs, but they had "unorthodox" views on the Prophets, reminiscent of the Samaritans' view on the matter:

> *Panarion 30 18:4*
> They acknowledge Abraham, Isaac and Jacob, Moses and Aaron—and Joshua the son of Nun simply as Moses' successor, though he is of no importance. But after these they acknowledge no more of the prophets, but even anathematize David and Solomon and make fun of them. Similarly they disregard Isaiah and Jeremiah, Daniel and Ezekiel, Elijah and Elisha; for they pay them no heed and blaspheme their prophecies, but accept only the Gospel.

They rejected the other prophets because, for them, the Christ is the only prophet, in the human form of Jesus, who merited to be called "Son of God" by his righteousness (*Panarion* 30 18:5–6). As Methodius of Olympus records, "and with regard to the Spirit, such as the Ebionites, who contend that the prophets spoke only by their own power" (*Symposium on Virginity*, 8.10). Their unorthodoxy goes beyond the Prophets, though, for it seems that they did not entirely accept the Torah as being from God.

> *Panarion 30 18:7–9*
> Nor do they accept Moses' Pentateuch in its entirety; they reject certain sayings. When you say to them, of eating meat, 'Why did Abraham serve the angels the calf and the milk? Why did Noah eat meat, and why was he told to by God, who said, 'Slay and eat?' Why did Isaac and Jacob sacrifice to God—Moses too, in the wilderness?' he will disbelieve those things and will say, 'What need for me to read what is in the Law, when the Gospel has come?' 'Well, how do you know about Moses and Abraham? I know you admit that they exist, and that you put them down as

righteous, and your own ancestors.' Then he will answer, 'Christ has revealed this to me,' and will blaspheme most of the legislation, and Samson, David, Elijah, Samuel, Elisha and the rest.

They read back into the text their vegetarianism and opposition to sacrifices. This is similar to some views in Islam and Samaritanism, i.e. that the Torah was corrupted at some point and needed to be "corrected" by a prophet. For the Muslims, this was Muhammad, for the Ebionites it was the Christ-infused Jesus. The Clementine literature regards *any* anthropomorphic material in the Torah to be a corruption of God's own words.[4]

The Ebionites migrated to Pella, a town in the Decapolis, in modern Syria, after the war with Rome (*Panarion* 30 2:7), it is there that they encountered the Nazoraens, or had they been in contact all along?

The Ebionites are related to two other Judeo-Christian groups mentioned by the Church Fathers, the Nasaraeans and the Nazoraeans. These might be names for the same group in different places and times. The term *Ebionite* seems to be a pejorative term, used by heresiologists and not by the community themselves. It seems more likely that they would use some variation of *Nazarene* (as we discuss below). These are likely chronological variations on the same group. This is especially important, because Jesus is called *Ha Notsri* (the Nazarene) in the Talmud. In other words, what we have is a *sectarian identification* for Jesus in the Talmud.

The Nazoraeans were either active after or contemporaneous with the Nasaraeans and held similar beliefs to them (*Panarion* 29 1:1). They did not use the name "Christians" (*Panarion* 19 1:3–4). However, there might be a connection to the Therapeutae, mentioned by Philo in his *De Vita Contemplativa*. The Therapeutae were an ascetic group in Alexandria, Egypt, who were later regarded by the Church Fathers as the first order of Christian monks. Epiphanius describes the connection to the Therapeutae.

> *Panarion 29 5:1*
> If you enjoy study and have read the passage about them in Philo's historical writings, in his book entitled 'Jessaeans,' you can find that, in giving his account of their way of life and their hymns and describing their monasteries in the vicinity of the Marean marsh, Philo described none other than Christians.

---

4. C.f. *Clementine Homilies* 2.38.1; 45–52; 18.19–20 The anthropomorphic references to God have caused other Jewish thinkers to re-analyze those portions of Torah, most notably Moses Maimonides in the Middle Ages, who metaphorized those references, instead of deleting them.

However, it is unlikely that this group was Christian at all. In Section III, Philo describes the group as being widely spread throughout the Greco-Roman world:

> Now this class of persons may be met with in many places, for it was fitting that both Greece and the country of the barbarians should partake of whatever is perfectly good; and there is the greatest number of such men in Egypt, in every one of the districts, or nomes, as they are called, and especially around Alexandria; and from all quarters those who are the best of these therapeutae proceed on their pilgrimage to some most suitable place as if it were their country, which is beyond the Mareotic lake.

The Therapeutae were regarded as proto-Christians by the early Church Fathers. However, their teachings seem to resemble the Gnosticism of the early Jesus movement. They lived simple lives, with a vow of poverty. They lived contemplative, ascetic lives, with isolation, study of Scriptures and prayers. They gathered together on the Sabbath.

The term "Nazoraean" comes from the Greek, *Nazaraioi* and is used by Epiphanius to distinguish them from the *Naziraioi*, the nazirites. These both are distinguished from the *Nasaraioi*, the Nasaraeans. Jerome calls the group of *Nazoraioi* the *Nazorei* or *Nazareni*.[5]

The New Testament uses the term *Nazoraios* and sometimes *Nazarenos*, the latter is preferred by Mark[6], whereas Matthew and John use the former.[7] Luke-Acts uses both terms, depending on when he is following Mark as a source[8] and in other contexts the form *Nazaraios*.[9] The term *Nazarenos* is only applied to Jesus, not his disciples. Matthew connects *Nazoraios* to Nazareth in Matthew 2:23. Christians were called *Nazoraens*, in Hebrew, *notsrim*. The term *Nazoraios*, then, is what Matthew uses to connect Jesus to Nazareth, but also used by Acts 24:5 to describe Judeo-Christians, even though very few would have been from Nazareth. Perhaps the village became a place of importance in early Christianity. All of these terms are related to the Hebrew *nezter* (root, branch). How did the term evolve? First, Christians were called Nazoraeans (*Panarion* 29.1.2–3). Later, the Christians became called Iesaeans, which Epiphanius identifies with the

---

5. Kinzig. "The Nazoreans" p. 468.

6. 1:24; 10:47; 14:67; 16:6

7. Matthew 2:23; 26:71; John 18:5,7; 19:19

8. Luke 4:34; 24:19

9. Luke 18:37; Acts 2:22; 3:6; 4:10; 6:14; 22:8; 24:5; 26:9

Essenes of Philo's work. In Antioch, the term *Christian* began to be used. A group, called the Nazoraeans, split from the Iessaeans and became known by that name.[10]

First, though, Philo spent time with the Nazoraeans in Alexandria, celebrating Passover with them. They had some unique customs, such as fasting throughout the holiday of Passover (*Panarion* 29 5:1–3). They followed Jewish law as the other Judeo-Christian sects did (*Panarion* 29 5:4). Epiphanius claims that they accepted the teaching of Jesus by the preaching of the Apostle Mark in Egypt and came to believe in him:

> *Panarion 29 5:6*
> For by hearing just Jesus' name, and seeing the miracles performed by the hands of the apostles, they came to faith in Jesus themselves. And since they found that he had been conceived at Nazareth and brought up in Joseph's home, and for this reason is called 'Jesus the Nazoraean' in the Gospel—as the apostles say, 'Jesus the Nazoraean, a man approved by signs and wonders,' and so on—they adopted this name, so as to be called Nazoreans.

There are two possibilities here. First, the Jessaeans became "Nazoraeans" because Jesus "the Nazoraean" was from Nazareth. It seems more likely that the other meaning is more likely, considering they were not from Galilee and would have no reason to identify with Jesus' hometown. It's more likely that they identified the name "Jesus" with the Christ above. This name should not be confused with the *nazirites*, as made explicit by Epiphanius:

> *Panarion 29 5:7*
> Not 'Nazirites'—that means 'consecrated persons.' Anciently this rank belonged to firstborn sons and men who had been dedicated to God. Samson was one, and others after him, and many before him. Moreover, John the Baptist too was one of these same persons who were consecrated to God, for 'He drank neither wine nor strong drink.' (This regimen, an appropriate one for their rank, was prescribed for such persons.)

It seems the name "Nazoraeans" was used frequently to describe *all* Christians, because Jesus was "a Nazoraen." This is even attested in the New Testament (Acts 24:5), which is a later text and might show that this term was gaining some popularity, as was Christian. Epiphanius is quick to point out that this does *not* mean that the Apostles shared in the Nazoraens'

---

10. Kinzig. "The Nazoreans" p. 479.

heresy (29 6:3). The Apostles accepted the term because it was an homage to Jesus *of Nazareth*, according to Epiphanius. He references Matthew's claim that the Prophets awaited a man, ""He will be called a Nazarene" (Matt. 2:23), although there is no direct reference to this in the Tanakh, although it might be an allusion to Isaiah 60:1–2, which uses the word, *netzer*, a shoot or branch.

Epiphanius complains about the most peculiar of linguistic complaints. He complains that everyone is being called a Christian these days. This includes Manichaeans, Marcionites, Gnostics, among all sorts of heretics, some of whom do not even profess basic Christian belief (*Panarion* 29 6:6). It is improper for the Nazoraeans themselves to keep this name since they do not fully follow Christ but are "Jews in every way and nothing else" (*Panarion* 29 7:1).

The Nazoraeans used the same writings as the Jews did:

> *Panarion 29 7:2, 4*
> They use not only the New Testament but the Old Testament as well, as the Jews do. For they do not repudiate the legislation, the prophets, and the books which are called *Writings* by the Jews and by themselves. They have no different views but confess everything in full accord with the doctrine of the Law and like the Jews, except that they are supposedly believers in Christ. They are perfectly versed in the Hebrew language, for the entire Law, the prophets, and the so-called *Writings*—I mean the poetic books, *Kings*, *Chronicles*, *Esther* and all the rest—are read in Hebrew among them, as of course they are among the Jews.

They appear more "orthodox" in feel, acknowledging that God created all things and that God is one, although "his Son is Jesus Christ", indicating a proto-orthodox[11] bent (*Panarion* 29 7:3). It seems they were both closer to Christians and Jews than the Ebionites:

> *Panarion 29 7:5*
> They are different from Jews, and different from Christians, only in the following ways. They disagree with Jews because of their belief in Christ; but they are not in accord with Christians because they are still fettered by the Law—circumcision, the Sabbath, and the rest.

---

11. The term "proto-orthodox" is used by some to indicate the group of Christians who held beliefs similar to what would become the orthodox Catholic Church later.

Epiphanius does not know the Christology of this group, whether they are proto-Orthodox or Cerinthian, like the Ebionites. They were located throughout the Decapolis in Syria (*Panarion* 29 7:7). This was their origin, after the Jerusalem community fled the city in the Jewish War with Rome:

> *Panarion 29 7:8*
> For that was its place of origin, since all the disciples had settled in Pella after their remove from Jerusalem—Christ having told them to abandon Jerusalem and withdraw from it because of the siege it was about to undergo. And they settled in Peraea for this reason and, as I said, lived their lives there. It was from this that the Nazoraean sect had its origin.

The Nazoraeans were not regarded well by the Jews:

> *Panarion 29 9:2–3*
> Yet to the Jews they are very much enemies. Not only do Jewish people bear hatred against them; they even stand up at dawn, at midday, and toward evening, three times a day when they recite their prayers in the synagogues, and curse and anathematize them—saying three times a day, 'God curse the Nazoraeans.' For they harbor a further grudge against them, if you please, because despite their Jewish origin, they preach that Jesus is the Christ—something that is the opposite of those who are still Jews and have not accepted Jesus.

Like the Ebionites, they possessed a Gospel in Hebrew, which Epiphanius calls "Matthew." It's quite possible that they did not include the genealogies at the beginning of the canonical version (*Panarion* 29 9:4).

What we likely have here, is a chronological spectrum and theological continuum among Judeo-Christians, which is viewed from the point of view of the heresiologists. This means that some Judeo-Christians were closer to the proto-orthodox Christian group in their Christology and belief, while some were not. The Judeo-Christian community stems back to Jesus himself in the Nasaraean group, which later became known as Nazoraean or Ebionite *to the heresiologists*.

The Rabbis knew the Judeo-Christians well, both in Palestine and Babylonia, and had many interactions with them. There are many references throughout the Talmuds to the *minim* or Judeo-Christians as they are called. The Rabbis even did not allow fasting on Sunday. Some Rabbis said this was due to the *Notsrim* (*Ta'anit* 27b).

However, few Christians are mentioned by name, other than the famous heretic [*min*], Jacob of Kefar Sekaniah, sometimes called Jacob Mina, "Jacob the min" (*Megillah* 23b). We have seen Jacob before in our journey; he was known as a faith healer. It is hard to establish a date for his life, but Hertford thinks he lived around 130 CE, but he converses with Judah Ha Nasi, which would be earlier in the 2nd century.

Jacob was on good terms with some of the Rabbis, because his questions to them are preserved in the Talmud, meaning he was allowed to discuss issues with them in their circles:

> *Megillah 23a*
> "Jacob the Min asked Rabbi Judah: What do the six of the Day of Atonement represent? — He replied: The six who stood at the right of Ezra and the six who stood at his left, as it says, And Ezra the scribe stood upon a pulpit of wood which they had made for the purpose . . . "

On one occasion, we even saw that he taught a *halakhah* to Rabbi Eliezer ben Hyrcanus, who accepted his teaching in the name of Jesus as acceptable. For this reason, Rabbi Eliezer was excommunicated by his fellow Rabbis.

Besides Jacob, there are many other stories of Christians as healers in the Talmud. There are countless regulations about how to handle *minim* within the community. The text of the liturgy was changed to include a "blessing" (really a curse) against them in public services. This was meant to "weed out" any *minim* in the community, who, logically would not be able to curse themselves as the public prayer leader. There are regulations about how to handle their books, Torah scrolls written by them, among a myriad of other regulations, set in place by the Rabbis.

The Judeo-Christians slowly died out and seem to have disappeared at some point in history. It seems the Babylonian rabbis still knew of them in the 5th and 6th centuries CE, but no other traces remain after that time. The non-Jewish Christian movement quickly outpaced the Judeo-Christians and did their best to stamp out any evidence of them in the historical record. We have lost their texts, their histories, and voices. Luckily, traces can be detected in the sources that do remain.

The Lessons Learned from Jesus by the Rabbis

T HERE ARE A NUMBER of other references in the Talmud that refer to Jesus, but in a non-historical way, meaning they cannot be used to make any inferences about his life. However, this does not mean that they are completely useless. In fact, they can best be understood as *lessons* that the Rabbis learned from their memories of the historical Jesus.

In Berakhot, a tractate dedicated to the various blessings recited by Jews at different occasions, we find a number of midrashic or *aggadic* statements. These are non-legal teachings on a variety of issues. Here the Rabbis are interpreting a verse, Psalms 144:14, which describes the leaders of the people of Israel. The Rabbis extract from the verse a series of characteristics that their leaders should embody. They should be "laden with mitzvot", without "breach", as their faction of Sages aspires to be. They learn from a variety of biblical characters how their leaders should *not* behave. The thrust of the message is to avoid schisms and evildoing. The last reference is to Jesus the Nazarene, who sinned in public, and caused others to sin. This should be read in the context of the exhortation against breaking away in the earlier part of the *sugya*. I think the *sugya* teaches that the Rabbis wanted to avoid sectarianism in the aftermath of the war with Rome and the destruction of the Temple. They wanted to preserve the Jewish people together as one and they saw Jesus as doing the opposite of that. This is a reflection on the Judeo-Christians, more than Jesus, since they maintained a separate, sectarian identity, after the war, when the Rabbis began the process of reconstruction.

Berakhot 17a-b

When the Sages took leave of the study hall of Rav Ḥisda, and some say it was **the study hall of Rabbi Shmuel bar Naḥmani, they would say to him the following,** in accordance with the verse: **"Our leaders are laden,** there is no breach and no going forth and no outcry in our open places" (Psalms 144:14).

Our leaders are laden. Rav and Shmuel, and some say Rabbi Yoḥanan and Rabbi Elazar, disputed the proper understanding of this verse. **One said: Our leaders in Torah are laden with mitzvot. And one said: Our leaders in Torah and mitzvot are laden with suffering.**

"There is no breach"; that our faction of Sages **should not be like the faction of David, from which Ahitophel emerged,** who caused a breach in the kingdom of David.

"And no going forth"; that our faction should not be like the faction of Saul, from which Doeg the Edomite emerged, who set forth on an evil path.

"And no outcry"; that our faction should not be like the faction of Elisha, from which Geihazi emerged.

"In our open places"; that we should not have a child or student who overcooks his food in public, i.e., who sins in public and causes others to sin, **as** in the well-known case of **Jesus the Nazarene.**

A second, famous episode is found in Gittin, which deals with divorce overall, but here deviates on a midrashic teaching. Here we find the story of Onkelos the proselyte, who was an important figure in early rabbinic Judaism. He became so prominent to be commissioned to translate the Torah into Aramaic in the *Targum*, the official Rabbinic commentary of the Torah into the vernacular.

The story relates his conversion to Judaism, as he raises various historical figures from the dead and asks them questions. He first raises Titus, the general who conquered Jerusalem, and asks "Who is most important to you now?" Titus responds that it is the Jewish people. Onkelos then asks if he should convert. Titus discourages him, because there are numerous commandments to fulfill and that Onkelos will not be able to do so. Titus uses Scriptural language in rabbinic rhetoric to support his claim that Onkelos will become a leader if he defeats the Jewish People. Onkelos asks each person what their punishment is, which results in a graphic description. Titus is burned every day and his ashes are scattered over the sea.

Gittin 56b-57a

The Gemara relates: **Onkelos bar Kalonikos, the son of Titus's sister, wanted to convert** to Judaism. **He went** and **raised Titus** from the grave **through necromancy,** and **said to him: Who is** most **important in that world** where you are now? Titus **said to him: The Jewish people.** Onkelos asked him: **Should I** then **attach** myself **to them** here in this world? Titus **said to him: Their commandments are numerous, and you will not be able to fulfill them.** It is best that you do as follows: **Go out and battle against them in that world, and you will become the chief, as it is written: "Her adversaries** [tzareha] **have become the chief"** (Lamentations 1:5), which means: **Anyone who distresses** [meitzer] **Israel will become the chief.** Onkelos **said to him: What is the punishment of that man,** a euphemism for Titus himself, in the next world? Titus **said to him: That which he decreed against himself, as he undergoes the following: Every day his ashes are gathered, and they judge him, and they burn him, and they scatter him over the seven seas.**

Onkelos was unsatisfied with Titus' answer and raises Balaam from the dead and asks him the same question, receiving the same answer. Balaam answers the same as Titus and adds that Onkelos should not convert and should not "seek their welfare." Balaam is punished by being boiled in semen, due to his causing Israel to sin by having relations with the daughters of Moab.

Onkelos then **went and raised Balaam** from the grave **through necromancy. He said to him: Who is** most **important in that world** where you are now? Balaam **said to him: The Jewish people.** Onkelos asked him: **Should I** then **attach** myself **to them** here in this world? Balaam **said to him: You shall not seek their peace or their welfare all the days** (see Deuteronomy 23:7). Onkelos **said to him: What is the punishment of that man,** a euphemism for Balaam himself, in the next world? Balaam **said to him:** He is cooked **in boiling semen,** as he caused Israel to engage in licentious behavior with the daughters of Moab..

Finally, Onkelos raises Jesus the Nazarene, asking the same questions. Jesus responds to Onkelos' question, "Their welfare you shall seek, their misfortune you shall not seek, for anyone who touches them is regarded as if he were touching the apple of his eye" indicating that Onkelos should join the Jewish People. Jesus is punished with boiling excrement, because he "mocked the words of the Sages."

Perhaps this could indicate something about the historical Jesus, expanding on his great sin, which was to mock the Sages. How exactly this happened is not recorded for us, but it must be a reference to his teaching, which contradicted the Rabbis' understanding of theology and law.

The *sugya* does tell us quite a bit about how the Rabbis thought about the Judeo-Christians, as the latter part of the *sugya* indicates that there is a difference between Jewish and non-Jewish sinners. Non-Jews do not look out for the welfare of Israel, whereas Jewish sinners *do*, even though they sinned.

> Onkelos then **went** and **raised Jesus the Nazarene** from the grave **through necromancy.** Onkelos **said to him: Who is** most **important in that world** where you are now? Jesus **said to him: The Jewish people.** Onkelos asked him: **Should I** then **attach** myself **to them** in this world? Jesus **said to him: Their welfare you shall seek, their misfortune you shall not seek,** for **anyone who touches them** is regarded **as if he were touching the apple of his eye** (see Zechariah 2:12).
>
> Onkelos **said to him: What is the punishment of that man,** a euphemism for Jesus himself, in the next world? Jesus **said to him:** He is punished **with boiling excrement. As the Master said: Anyone who mocks the words of the Sages will be sentenced to boiling excrement.** And this was his sin, as he mocked the words of the Sages. The Gemara comments: **Come** and **see the difference between the sinners of Israel and the prophets of the nations of the world.** As Balaam, who was a prophet, wished Israel harm, whereas Jesus the Nazarene, who was a Jewish sinner, sought their well-being.
>
> To conclude the story of Kamtza and bar Kamtza and the destruction of Jerusalem, the Gemara cites a *baraita*. It **is taught: Rabbi Elazar says: Come and see how great is the power of shame, for the Holy One, Blessed be He, assisted bar Kamtza,** who had been humiliated, **and** due to this humiliation and shame **He destroyed His Temple and burned His Sanctuary.**

These passages reveal how the Rabbis thought about Jesus and the Judeo-Christians in the centuries after the life of Jesus. It is often said that the separation between Judaism and Christianity took centuries to complete and the texts in the Talmud share that view. The Judeo-Christians were kept within arms' length, as they were still Jews, even if sinners, according to the Rabbis' perspective.

Conclusion

THE JESUS OF THE Talmud is a completely different Jesus from the one that we have come to know from Christian sources. He is deviant, scandalous, fraudulent, and somehow tragic at the same time, yet not unlikeable. He comes from a world vastly different from our own, and even from the world that Christians ascribe to him. His was not the world of Roman domination, not yet. He grew up knowing Jewish sovereignty. He fled to Egypt with his teacher when the Jewish king lashed out against the Pharisees and persecuted them.

His parents were Miriam and Pantera, as the earliest stratum of tradition identifies. He must have been from a well-to-do family to be invited into the highest rank of rabbinic culture. He must have known the Torah well and mastered the rabbinic curriculum to have merited a position as a student of Yehoshua ben Peraḥyah, the leading Rabbi of his age. His teacher trusted him well, even leaving with him to Egypt, for some years, before returning with a different Jesus.

Something happened to Jesus in Egypt. That "something" is not preserved in history. Yet, he left Egypt a changed man. He must have run into Gnostic teachers in Alexandria, among all sorts of religious sects. We know he was an inquisitive mind; we have seen the teachings preserved in his name. Something pushed him to question the boundaries of the orthodoxy of his day and to part ways with his trusted teacher.

Whatever happened, he was not a part of the rabbinic circle when he returned to Israel. He began teaching *against* the Rabbis. He proclaimed the Torah was altered, changed, from its original holy form. The Pharisees and scribes had *not* preserved the Torah of Moses, as he understood it. This rebellion would cost him dearly, it would cost him his life.

He was arrested by the Jewish court and tried for inciting others to idolatry and for sorcery, two capital offenses. Both were serious accusations that resulted in his death. No one came to defend him in the end. He was left without a favorable witness to defend his teaching or character and brought to be executed.

This is the rabbinic story of Jesus' life, as preserved by the Rabbis of the Talmud, Sephardic Rabbis and writers throughout the ages.

As different as the Talmudic narrative *seems*, it is likely that the Rabbis knew the Christian texts, in some form, particularly the Gospel of John. There are several allusions to his life in the Gospels in the Talmudic narrative such as the details of Jesus' family are shared, Jesus' Torah teachings and his circle of disciples, healing in the name of Jesus, Jesus' execution on the fourteenth of Nisan, the day before Passover.[1]

The Babylonian Talmud mentions harsher details about Jesus (being a bastard, a magician, the bad disciple, the idolater, his punishment in the afterlife). In the Jerusalem Talmud, the focus is on the healing powers of Jesus' disciples and the sect that lived on after him, particularly their use of magic, as interpreted by the Rabbis. In Israel, the Rabbis encountered Christians and were concerned with the origins of Christianity and their interaction with it. Because the Rabbis in Babylon did not interact with Christians, to the same extent, they felt more liberty to express their uncensored opinions and their story about him.[2]

Even so, his story did not end there. His teaching lived on, as students continued to accept his understanding of Judaism and the Torah. The answer lies beyond the Talmud, beyond any sources we have. We can speculate as to what happened.

Jesus was a Nasaraean. These followers continued after his death. In the 1st century CE, Jesus' followers began to have visionary experiences of him, most notably, Paul of Tarsus. It's not clear how Paul heard about Jesus, or if he was even thinking of the same man when he spoke of the "risen Lord" and his "gospel." After spending time in the desert, in Arabia, Paul found the community of Nazoraeans in Jerusalem, a descendant of the Nasaraeans. The leaders of the community were Cephas, Jacob, and John, who

---

1. Schäfer, *Jesus in the Talmud*, p. 123.
2. Schäfer, *Jesus in the Talmud*, p. 102.

reluctantly admitted Paul into their fellowship, in exchange for a collection of offerings for the poor in Jerusalem. That story is best left for another day.

What the Talmud teaches us about Jesus is how a Jewish heretic became the founder of the world's largest religion. The Rabbis knew Jesus when he lived and preserved their memories in the way that they preserved *all* historical memories, as proofs or sources for legal argumentation in formulating the halakhot of how to live and observe Jewish law in a variety of situations. Jesus' story in the Talmud occurs where it should, in the discussion of the minutiae of how capital offenses are tried, *because that is a major component of Jesus' story in the Talmud*. The Rabbis remember a rebellious son, a lost heretic, one who abandoned the Torah for the ways of gnosis and magic, and perhaps even a man who struggled with mental illness. The latter point is impossible to know for certain, but it is attested in both Rabbinic and Gospel traditions, which allows us to say that Jesus was *regarded* as not mentally well by at least *some* of his interlocutors during his life.

The Talmud also tells us who Jesus was *not*. He was not a messiah, nor claimed the throne of Israel for himself or anyone else. He was not apocalyptic. He did not want the world to end, because he was "close to the government", one who benefited from the status quo, as did many other Rabbis. He did not raise an army, nor march on any enemies. His was an entirely *internal* Jewish affair. He lived under Jewish rulers, Alexander Jannaeus, Salome Alexandra, Hyrcanus II, and possibly, Aristobulus II. The record of Jesus' teaching provides a glimpse into why he annoyed the powers-that-be so much in Jerusalem. He questioned the foundation of Pharisaic belief by questioning the legitimacy of the Torah itself. The Sadducees did not accept the oral law, which could be tolerated to a certain extent, but to question the validity of the Torah of Moses was another matter. Jesus was also *too* close to magic to be palatable to the Pharisees, who sought to "reign in" the practice of magic among Israel.

Why should the Talmud be taken seriously as a source for learning about the historical Jesus? Because it preserves the only alternative tradition. Every other source for the historical Jesus ultimately stems from the Gospel of Mark. Matthew and Luke debate with Mark about the finer points of Jesus' life, but accept the overall structure. John is different, yes, but preserves few historical details. The Gnostic Gospels also depend on the canonical tradition, in one way or another, to contest the details of Jesus' life within the structure and chronology of Mark. The Gospel of Thomas provides a wealth of information about Jesus' teaching, but not much about his historical life, but it can be regarded as an alternative tradition.

Modern scholarship follows in the footsteps of Mark as well. Beginning with Albert Schweitzer, until the scholars of today, the majority of scholars of the historical Jesus are *New Testament* scholars and begin with an underlying assumption that the Gospels contain some historical record about Jesus' life. Most importantly, they accept the chronology of the Gospels without much thought as to why.

Determining exactly when Jesus lived has never been an exact science. Without a discovery of a new library of documents, we are left with the scant sources we have now. However, it would be unfair to consider an issue without investigating both sides of that issue. The Talmud is often considered to be too old to provide any reliable information about the historical Jesus, but this relies on faulty logic, that "older equals better." This is not necessarily the case, but is often assumed to be so. It also discredits oral tradition and cultures that have a strong oral history, such as the case was with the Jews of the 1st century CE.

Ultimately, the quest for the historical Jesus is an unattainable one, due to the lack of evidence. However, this book has presented a case to *consider* the Talmud's account. It has presented all of the information that can be gleaned about Jesus and his followers from the Talmud's pages. Whether or not it is an accurate picture remains to be seen, but should be considered by all.

Glossary

Aggadah: refers to sections of the Mishnah and Talmud that are non-legal in nature including biblical exegesis, folklore, historical anecdotes, moral exhortations, and practical advice.

Amoraim:

Ashkenazic: a Jewish diaspora community in Central and Eastern Europe.

Bar Kokhba: leader of a second century CE against the Romans

Baraita (pl. baraitot): Aramaic "outside", a tradition in Jewish law not included in the final text of the Mishnah, often used in the Gemara in argumentation about a specific halakhah.

Ebionites: heresiological name for a Judeo-Christian sect in the first century CE and onwards. Derived from Hebrew, evyonim, poor ones.

Gemara: Aramaic, to finish, refers to rabbinic analysis and commentary to the Mishnah redacted in both the Jerusalem and Babylonian Talmuds between the fifth and sixth centuries CE.

Gnosticism: a term used to describe a variety of beliefs shared among Jewish and Christians groups, usually with some emphasis on *gnosis* (knowledge) in salvation, a shared cosmology with some negativity usually assigned to the physical world.

Halakhah: Hebrew, walking, refers to the derivation of Jewish law from the written and oral Torah.

Hasmonean: a ruling dynasty in Judea and the surrounding area from 140 BCE to 37 BCE.

Josephus: a first century Roman-Jewish historian. His two most famous works are *The Antiquities of the Jews* and *The Jewish War*.

Maḥloket: a halakhic, legal dispute between two rabbinic authorities

Mamzer: Hebrew, bastard, a person born of forbidden relationships or incest

Mandaeans: a Gnostic religion that venerates John the Baptist as a prophet that still exists in parts of Iran and Iraq.

Metatron: an angel in Jewish cosmology

Moses Maimonides: influential Spanish philosopher and Jewish theologian who wrote works of Jewish philosophy and Jewish law

Nasaraeans: a 1st century sect mentioned by Epiphanius that pre-dated and post-dated the life of Jesus.

Nasi: Hebrew title meaning "prince" which was the leader of the Sanhedrin in the Second Temple period

Nazoraeans: reference to sect of Judeo-Christians in the first century CE and beyond who observed Jewish law and held heterodox views about the person of Jesus

Mishnah: written compendium of Jewish oral law

Pirke Avot: a section of the Mishnah with no legal material and only aggadic statements

Sage: another word for "Rabbi"

Sephardic: refers to Jews who origins lie in medieval Spain.

Sugya: a part of the Gemara, the "building block" of the structure of the Talmud

Talmud: collection of the Mishnah and Gemara

Tannaim: "repeaters" those who memorized sections of the Mishnah for study in rabbinic yeshivot

Tosefta: supplementary collection of oral laws that were not included in the Mishnah

Yeshivah: rabbinic study hall for learning oral laws

Bibliography

Alexander, "Incantations and Books of Magic," in *The History of the Jewish People in the Age of Jesus Christ*, edited by Geza Vermes et al., 342-379. Edinburgh: T & T Clark, 1986.

Bader, Gershom. *The Jewish Spiritual Heroes: The Lives and Works of the Rabbinical Teachers from the Beginning of the Great Synagogue to the Final Completion of the Talmud: Seven Centuries of Jewish Thought (3 Vols)*. Pardes, 1940.

Barton, George et al. "Rechabites." *The Jewish Encyclopedia*. New York: Funk & Wagnalls, 1901-1906.

Brashear, William M.. "The Greek Magical Papyri: an Introduction and Survey; Annotated Bibliography (1928-1994)" in *Heidentum: Die religiösen Verhältnisse in den Provinzen: Die religiösen Verhältnisse in den Provinzen*, edited by Wolfgang Haase, 3380-3684. Berlin, Boston: De Gruyter, 2016.

Carrier, Richard. *On the Historicity of Jesus: Why We Might have Reason for Doubt*. Sheffield: Sheffield Phoenix, 2014.

Collins, John J. "The Son of Man and the Saints of the Most High in the Book of Daniel." *Journal of Biblical Literature* 93, no. 1 (1974): 50–66.

Dalman, Gustaf. *Jesus Christ in the Talmud, Midrash, Zohar, and the Liturgy of the Synagogue*. Cambridge, 1893.

Dykstra, Tom. *Mark Canonizer of Paul: A New Look at Intertextuality in Mark's Gospel*. OCABS, 2012.

Ehrman, Bart and Zlatko Plese. *The Other Gospels: Accounts of Jesus from Outside the New Testament*. Oxford University Press (2014).

Ellegard, Alvar. *Jesus: One Hundred Years Before Christ*. Abrams, 1999.

Elman, Yaakov. "Orality and the Redaction of the Babylonian Talmud." *Oral Tradition* 14/1 (1999) 52-99.

Epiphanius of Salamis. T*he Panarion of Epiphanius of Salamis: Book I*. Translated by Frank Williams. *Nag Hammadi and Manichaean Studies*, Volume: 63. Brill, 2008.

Faur, José. *The Gospel According to the Jews*. Moreshet Sepharad, 2012.

———. *The Horizontal Society: Understanding the Covenant and Alphabetic Judaism*. Academic Studies Press, 2010.

BIBLIOGRAPHY

Fishbane, Simcha. "'Most Women Engage in Sorcery': An Analysis of Female Sorceresses in the Babylonian Talmud", in *Deviancy in Early Rabbinic Literature: A Collection of Socio-Anthropological Essays,* edited by Simcha Fishbane, 84. Leiden & Boston: Brill, 2007.

Flavius Josephus. The Works of Flavius Josephus. Translated by. William Whiston, A.M. Auburn and Buffalo. John E. Beardsley. 1895.

Flavius Josephus. The Works of Flavius Josephus. Translated by. William Whiston, A.M. Auburn and Buffalo. John E. Beardsley. 1895.

Freedman, Harry. *The Talmud A Biography: Banned, Censored, and Burned. The Book They Couldn't Suppress.* Keren, 2014.

Giles, Glenn. Messianic Movements of the First Century. Trinity Theological Seminary. 2002. https://www.douglasjacoby.com/wp-content/uploads/2005/03/Mess.Movements. pdf.

Hauptman, Judith. *Re-Reading the Mishnah: A New Approach to Ancient Jewish Text.* Coronet Books, 2005.

Herford, R. Travers. *Christianity in the Talmud and Midrash.* London: Williams and Norgate, 1903.

Howard, George. *The Hebrew Gospel of Matthew.* Mercer University Press, 2005.

ibn Daud, Abraham. *The Book of Tradition (Sefer Ha-Qabbalah).* Jewish Publication Society, 2010.

Kampmeier, A. The Pre-Christian Nasareans (With Note by Dr. W. B. Smith). *The Open Court, 1913,* 2.

Kinzig, Wolfram. "The Nazoreans" in *Jewish Believers in Jesus,* edited by Oskar Skarsaune and Reidar Hvalvik, 463-487. Peabody: Hendrickson, 2007.

Klausner, Joseph. *Jesus of Nazareth: His Life, Times, and Teaching.* New York: MacMillan, 1920.

Kohler, Kaufmann. "Hemerobaptists." *The Jewish Encyclopedia.* New York: Funk & Wagnalls, 1901-1906.

Kraemer, David. "On the Reliability of Attributions in the Babylonian Talmud." *Hebrew Union College Annual* 60 (1989) 175–90.

Lauterbach, Jacob. *Rabbinic Essays.* Cincinnati: Hebrew Union College, 1951.

Lawrence, Michael. *Seventy: The Seventy Year Reverse Construction Thesis And Christians Before Jesus.* Independently published, 2020.

Lenowitz, Harris. *Jewish Messiahs: From the Galilee to Crown Heights.* Oxford University Press, 2001.

Maier, Johann. *Jesus von Nazareth in der talmudischen Uberlieferung,* Buchgesellschaft, 1978.

Meier, John P. *A Marginal Jew: Rethinking the Historical Jesus.* Doubleday (vols. 1-5), 1991-2016.

Mead, G.R.S. *Did Jesus Live 100 B.C.?* London: Theosophical Publishing Society, 1903.

Neusner, Jacob. "Judaic Uses of History in Talmudic Times." *History and Theory* 27, no. 4 (1988) 12–39.

———. *The Mishnah: An Introduction.* Rowman & Littlefield, 1994.

———. "Money-Changers in the Temple: the Mishnah's Explanation." *NTS* 35 (1989) 287–290.

New Revised Standard Version Bible, copyright © 1989 the Division of Christian Education of the National Council of the Churches of Christ in the United States of America. Used by permission. All rights reserved.

Oppenheimer, Aharon. Talmudic Literature as Historical Source. Frankel Center, the Frankel Institute for Advanced Judaic Studies, *Studying Jews* (2009) 17-20.

Orlov, Andrei A.. "Two Powers in Heaven . . . Manifested," in *Wisdom Poured Out Like Water: Studies on Jewish and Christian Antiquity in Honor of Gabriele Boccaccini,* edited by J. Harold Ellens et al., 351-364. Berlin, Boston: De Gruyter, 2018.

Patterson, Emma E. (2015) "Oral Transmission: A Marriage of Music, Language, Tradition, and Culture." *Musical Offerings* Vol. 6 : No. 1 , Article 2.

Pick, Bernard. *Jesus in the Talmud*. Chicago: Open Court Publishing Company, 1913.

Roberts, Alexander, James Donaldson, and A. Cleveland Coxe, eds. *Ante-Nicene Fathers,* Vol. 1. Translated by Alexander Roberts and William Rambaut. Buffalo: Christian Literature Publishing Co., 1885.

Saiman, Chaim. *Halakhah: Rabbinic Idea of Law*. Princeton University Press, 2018.

Salm, René. *NazarethGate*. American Atheist, 2015.

Sanders, E. P. *The Historical Figure of Jesus*. Lane The Penguin, 1993.

Schäfer, Peter. *Jesus in the Talmud*. Princeton University Press, 2007.

Schaff, Philip and Henry Wace, eds. *Nicene and Post-Nicene Fathers, Second Series*, Vol. 1. Translated by Arthur Cushman McGiffert. Buffalo, NY: Christian Literature Publishing Co., 1890.

Shechter, Solomon and Wilhelm Bacher. "Johanan B. Zakai." *The Jewish Encyclopedia*. New York: Funk & Wagnalls, 1901-1906.

Shechter, Solomon and A.S. Waldstein. "Judah B. Baba." *The Jewish Encyclopedia*. New York: Funk & Wagnalls, 1901-1906.

Sigal, Phillip. *The Halakhah of Jesus of Nazareth According to the Gospel of Matthew*. Brill Academic Publishers, 2008.

Smith, Morton. *Jesus the Magician: A Renowned Historian Reveals How Jesus was Viewed by His People*. Hampton Roads Publishing, 2014.

Tabor, James. *The Jesus Dynasty: The Hidden History of Jesus, His Royal Family, and the Birth of Christianity*. Simon & Schuster, 2007.

Tacitus. *Complete Works of Tacitus*. Translated by Alfred John Church, William Jackson Brodribb, and Sara Bryant. New York. : Random House, Inc. Random House, Inc., reprinted 1942.

Van Voorst, Robert. *Jesus outside the New Testament*. Wm. B. Eerdmans, 2000.

Vansina, Jan. *Oral Tradition As History*. Madison: University of Wisconsin Press, 1985.

Vermes, Geza, *Jesus the Jew: A Historian's Reading of the Gospels*, Minneapolis, Fortress, 1973.

Subject Index

Scripture Index

John

Acts

Galatians

DEAD SEA SCROLLS

RABBINIC WRITINGS

Mishnah

Shabbat

Ḥagigah

Makkot

Yevamot

Sotah

Pirke Avot

Sanhedrin

Yadayim

Mikva'ot

Avot De Rabbi Natan

Tosefta

Ḥullin

Made in the USA
Middletown, DE
05 November 2024

63960726R00106